Toward a
National Antitrust Policy

Information Problems and Antitrust

Papers from the
Fifteenth Conference on
Antitrust Issues in Today's Economy
New York, New York
March 4, 1976

and

Papers from the
Limited Briefing on
Antitrust in the United States
Frankfurt, Germany
October 29, 1975

Contents

Foreword

IN OCTOBER, 1975 and March, 1976, The Conference Board held two related programs on Antitrust Issues in Today's Economy. The first was a limited briefing session in Frankfurt, Germany, designed to help the Board's European Associates understand emerging U.S. antitrust concerns. The second was the Board's fifteenth annual one-day conference, "Antitrust Issues in Today's Economy."

Both programs were designed to be responsive to the requirements of the business community for a responsible and searching examination of emerging antitrust issues and current developments in the antitrust responsibilities of management. The sessions were planned and directed by Dr. Betty Bock, Director of the Board's Antitrust Research, but the papers, like all of those presented at the Board's antitrust conferences, represent the thinking of the individual participants.

The Conference Board is grateful to those who appeared on the programs, and to the corporate executives and their legal advisers whose continuing participation in the Board's antitrust meetings has contributed for so many years to their success.

March, 1976

DAVID G. MOORE
Executive Vice President,
Research

TOWARD A NATIONAL ANTITRUST POLICY

Data, Information and Antitrust: An Introduction

Betty Bock

ANTITRUST POLICY, and the enterprise system to which it is dedicated, represents a political and social philosophy, a series of statutes and judicial decisions, a public enforcement program, a myriad of private enforcement actions, and deep Congressional concern. It also represents an object of study by political scientists, economists and students of the form and goals of the United States economy.

Beginning in the 1890's as specific legislation designed to protect regional and local businesses from the growing power of national trusts, antitrust has been expanded through new laws and judicial concepts to become a part of our national purpose and of our methods of moving toward a humane and feasible economic and social order.

In proscribing attempts to monopolize and agreements in restraint of trade by private firms, the antitrust laws, therefore, express the national value we place upon free and open markets as the best-known mechanism for allocating resources among alternative consumer needs. This is so, even though various segments of the economy are perceived as lying within the orbit of antitrust, while others are explicitly exempt from antitrust surveillance and, instead, put under the guidance of specific regulatory agencies.

But since antitrust is a multifaceted policy designed to apply to a complex of enterprise operations, the application of the laws to the "free" sectors of the economy and the exemptions for the "regulated" sectors are under constant revision by the enforcement agencies, the courts, and by Congress. Meanwhile, other national goals, such as those concerned with environment, equal employment opportunity, product safety, and other social legislation, must also be taken into account by those concerned with the enterprise system and the maximizing of market opportunity for business and market choice for consumers.

What these broad areas of antitrust and exemption from antitrust mean for the future of the economy and for specific sectors of the economy comes into question, sometimes in clear-cut and sometimes in implicit form, whenever the meaning of enterprise legislation is under reconsideration, as it is currently.

But reconsideration of enterprise legislation and its relation to other laws requires appropriate information so that understanding of the paradoxes in the nature of competition and in our perceptions of it may be clarified by common vocabulary and common understanding of policy and program alternatives. Planned against this background, The Conference Board's fifteenth annual one-day program on "Antitrust Issues in Today's Economy," held in

March, 1976, was designed to focus on national antitrust policy and the information problems that underlie attempts to apply this policy in a complex and rapidly changing economy.

But raw data or isolated sets of words and numbers do not necessarily represent information, unless they are congruent with an underlying reality and represent a meaningful method of viewing that reality. And when reality is complex, it is not always obvious what data can be processed to form valid and verifiable information, as contrasted with items of data that can only be re-arranged to produce more data.

The fact is that in today's highly articulate − and articulated − world, we are in danger of becoming addicted to data without examining the numbers and words we generate and the information we need to understand the relations between our resources and our goals.

Although these facts are true of all fields of knowledge, they have over the last few years become particularly significant for antitrust, because we are simultaneously concerned with new policy and with new programs designed to obtain information for antitrust and a wide range of other public-policy purposes. But the proposals for new laws and information have burgeoned so rapidly that underlying problems remain to be identified and resolved; e.g., problems concerning slippage among the meanings of the words "industries," "markets" and "companies"; slippage among concepts of sales and shipments plus transfers; and slippage in understanding of the differences between the categories in which data are collected and the markets in which competition, in fact, takes place. Such ambiguities can create false certainties and uncertainties and so feed controversies that could be lessened by new focus on information relevant to industrial fact and antitrust policy.

The formal morning and luncheon sessions of The Conference Board's March, 1976, conference were, therefore, concerned with national antitrust policy and information problems and antitrust. At the morning session, papers on antitrust policy were presented by Robert A. Nitschke, Assistant General Counsel, General Motors Corporation, and Peter O. Steiner, Professor of Economics and Law, University of Michigan. At the luncheon session, moderated by Frederick M. Rowe, of Kirkland, Ellis & Rowe in Washington, D.C., Kenneth W. Dam of the Law School, University of Chicago; Ira M. Millstein, of Weil, Gotshal & Manges in New York City; and Howard L. Siers, Assistant Comptroller, E.I. du Pont de Nemours & Company, carried on a discussion of problems of information and antitrust.

Toward a National Antitrust Policy? – 1

Robert A. Nitschke

I SUPPOSE EVERYONE agrees that the antitrust laws, in proscribing monopolizing and agreements in restraint of trade by private firms, express a national policy in favor of the free market system. Underlying the philosophy of antitrust is a recognition that the marketplace is the best mechanism for allocating resources and satisfying consumer demands. The market does this generally by rewarding the participant in the economic process according to his contribution. The reward for success and the penalty for failure in the rivalry for the consumer's patronage is the stimulus that makes the system work.

At the same time that we hold to these beliefs and treat private restraints upon this system as felonies, however, public restraints across vast areas of our economy are legion. Federal and state laws and regulations fix prices, regulate and restrict entry, and place law-enforced limitations upon services and products – restrictions which in most cases would be *per se* violations of the antitrust laws if done by private agreement.

While there is an increasing awareness of the evils of unnecessary regulation and its interference with the successful operation of our economy – an awareness which is in no small part due to the articulate and persistent efforts of attorneys in the Antitrust Division – the legislatures, both federal and state, have done virtually nothing to deregulate. Instead, they continue to impose additional regulations upon the marketplace – regulations which coerce individuals in their roles as consumers and producers.

The obvious need in this 86th year of the existence of our antitrust laws is for a reemphasis of – a rededication to – economic freedom through market processes. In contrast, current national antitrust policy, insofar as it is expressed in proposed legislation, seems to consist solely of proposals to toughen enforcement, adding penalty to penalty, almost as if the Sherman Act were not our landmark of economic freedom but the greatest failure of all time.

The proposed Criminal Justice Reform Act, for example, would authorize fines up to "twice the gross gain derived or twice the gross loss caused" by antitrust violations.[1] Another bill before Congress would add to existing penalties a forfeiture of 20 percent of the gross revenue of the company during the period of violation.[2]

The proposed Industrial Reorganization Act and the current oil industry bills would impose the harshest of antitrust remedies – divestiture – without requiring proof of any restrictive or monopolistic activity.[3] And finally we have the so-called "parens patriae" bills, which would allow 50 state attorneys general to bring federal antitrust class actions for citizens of their states. And, far more significantly, it would permit these attorneys general *and any other private plaintiff* to recover unlimited sums in antitrust class actions without the need to prove actual damages to individual members of the class.[4]

Apparently, then, the only national antitrust policy which seems to be taken seriously is one of continually imposing tougher and tougher antitrust penalties and remedies. I would like to discuss this trend and ask the basic question whether the movement toward ever-tougher sanctions is helping or hurting the operation of a free competitive market.

At the outset, I think we should properly consider whether market processes are working all that badly. From the statements continuously forthcoming from certain legislators and other critics, you would think we live under an economic system that is a total failure, riddled with price fixing and sucked dry by greedy monopolists. Yet all the evidence points to just the opposite conclusion.

I like to think of the words on the official seal of my own State of Michigan: "If you would seek a beautiful peninsula, look around you." If we will just look, we can see evidence all around us that the free market is working well for society and for consumers in the United States — and that the problems which do exist are apt to be the result of existing governmental interference, not the result of inadequate antitrust enforcement.

We have had over the years two strong, active antitrust enforcement agencies. They are staffed today with more able and talented personnel than ever before. The law imposes severe penalties, materially strengthened last year.[5] What evidence is there that these are insufficient deterrents?

No system of criminal justice is ever perfect, of course. There may always be some who escape the net. But in all other areas of law enforcement we recognize that the continued escalation of punitive remedies is ultimately counterproductive. We would undoubtedly deter more people if all crimes were capital offenses, but we recognize that society would pay a severe price if that were true. I suggest that, particularly in the area of private antitrust enforcement, we have already reached the point where our competitive system and our society are suffering from enforcement overkill. Let me zero in on this matter of private damage actions.

The generality and ambiguity of the antitrust laws has always meant that the kinds of cases brought largely determine the direction in which competition policy evolves. This is a task which demands the best of public servants. It requires wisdom, experience and an understanding of the market system. Like all who believe in the marketplace, I strongly support adequate funding to enable the antitrust agencies to enforce the law strictly and to maintain high standards of professionalism. Private enforcement, however, has too often led to anticompetitive policy determinations and has produced a juridical climate of antitrust uncertainty and caprice.

We must remember that the objective of a plaintiff in treble-damage cases is not necessarily the public interest, the proper working of the free market, the promotion of competition, or even consistency in the law. It is simply the advocacy of whatever interpretations, theories and approaches will produce a

4

money judgment for him. In fact, as several courts have pointed out, treble-damage cases are frequently generated by attorneys seeking "a golden harvest of fees," not by the named plaintiffs at all.[6] I am not blaming counsel for their entrepreneurial spirit, but simply calling attention to the fact that the objectives of such suits may be remote from antitrust.

It is sometimes said that the steadily increasing number of private antitrust suits is evidence of widespread violations of law, which only these private plaintiffs are able to combat. Isn't it possible rather that this growth in litigation may represent imbalances in the private antitrust remedy itself? Given the magnitude of potential recoveries (particularly in class actions) and the consequent pressures on defendants to settle and inducements for attorneys to sue, it may be that the current litigation explosion is simply a self-sustaining chain reaction which does not demonstrate the prevalence of violations.

Let us look at the private antitrust remedy from the standpoint of a defendant faced with invalid claims or a suit of questionable merit. And I might add that even our courts, which are traditionally willing to give a defendant the benefit of the doubt in other contexts, too often seem to assume that an antitrust defendant is guilty and liable — and that the only question is for how much.

If this defendant has been also sued by the Federal Government, he is faced with a procedural gauntlet that is unparalleled in our legal system. The Justice Department has two shots at him, one criminal and one civil — a questionable practice in itself. If the defendant wins the criminal case, he is still put to defending the same charges a second time. If he loses *either one* of the government cases, that adverse decision creates a *prima facie* case for private plaintiffs in subsequent suits. If the defendant wins *both* government cases, he derives no evidentiary benefit at all for future cases.

Typically, a defendant is then faced with multiple private suits — even multiple class actions — raising the same claim, and 40 to 50 suits at a time are not uncommon. If all these private cases are consolidated for trial, millions or even billions of dollars may be risked on the vote of six or twelve jurors. If the cases are tried separately, the defendant has to win all of them because a victory in any one will not be an estoppel in any other. If he loses any one, he will, as a practical matter, have difficulty defending the others, whether legally estopped or not, because he is before the court in the posture of an adjudged antitrust violator. In effect, antitrust defendants can be put in double jeopardy over and over again.

Moreover, when the innocent defendant gets to court in a treble-damage case, he finds there are strong pressures to bend the substantive law against him. There is a feeling (sometimes candidly expressed) that overall antitrust objectives are furthered by a plaintiff's victory, even if it leads to quixotic results in a particular case. Even more damaging is the tendency for substantive rules to shift from protection of the competitive process to protection of individual competitors. This is apt to occur because so often a treble-damage case involves a plaintiff who has lost business or failed.

In any competitive race, some win gold medals, some silver, some bronze — but some are just plain losers. Indeed the more swift and intense the pace, the more likely that some will falter and drop out altogether. It is only in cartels, which allocate customers and products and fix prices, that every competitor can be a winner. But Americans are compassionate people and compassionate juries and courts alike tend to confuse the inevitable losses occurring in a strongly competitive market with restraints upon competition itself.

The United States Supreme Court itself has exhibited this failing in a number of cases. For example, a newspaper distributor with an exclusive territory hikes prices. The publisher, reacting in the way a free market is supposed to function, appoints another distributor who introduces price competition. The price-hiking monopolist recovers damages for lost business because the court finds a combination between the publisher and the new distributor to hold down resale prices.[7]

In another case, a company operating nationally cut its prices in a local market in order to meet those of a vigorous and successful local company that has the largest share of the business. Because the national company did not reduce prices in other markets, it is held to be engaging in predatory discriminatory pricing and is penalized for the business taken away from its competitor.[8]

Perhaps the most striking illustration of this problem at the lower-court level was the trial judge's decision in *Telex-IBM* where $300 million in damages were assessed against the defendant for price competition to avoid losing a lawfully obtained market position.[9] Success in that instance required putting the most efficient company in quarantine to stop its continued vigorous competition. The fact that this particular decision was reversed does not eliminate the danger that its rationale will reappear. The irony is that in each of these cases the extension of the protection of the antitrust law to a private plaintiff reflected both hostility to price competition and indifference to resulting increases in consumer ·costs.

Another hazard for the defendant is the risk of uncertainty about the jury's view of the facts, particularly when inferences are allowed to be drawn from widely ranging circumstantial evidence admitted "subject to connection." For example, the rivalrous reactions of firms to each other's competitive moves may quite normally result in similar pricing and other competitive activity. Yet juries are allowed to infer a conspiracy from very little more than a common course of action. As one judge has noted, these theories of conspiracy "come dangerously close to precluding lawful pricing activity as a part of vigorous competition."[10]

Finally, the hazards for the defendant are not offset by any comparable risk to the plaintiff or his attorneys. Plaintiffs do not face staggering liabilities from an unforeseeable shift in interpretation of the law, a marginal violation, or just a plain wrong guess by the jury. They are not liable for lawyers' fees if they lose. And at any point along the road, the cost of plaintiff counsel's time is so considerably less than the cost to the defendant of discovery and trial that plaintiffs can often obtain a substantial nuisance settlement. Such settlements are frequently cheaper for the defendant than trying the case, even if he wins. It is small wonder then that we frequently see large settlement offers by defendants and further small wonder that there are so many private suits brought by people who have so much to gain and so little to lose.

This existing overkill would be magnified beyond belief if the recovery provisions of the so-called "parens patriae" bills were passed. Under these bills any private litigant, not just a state attorney general, could bring an action on behalf of an unlimited number of people and recover an aggregate fund in an unlimited amount without the necessity of demonstrating that he or anyone else had actually been injured. Proof by "statistical or sampling methods" would be permitted without regard to whether the damages recovered could, as a practical matter, be distributed to the putative class members.

Such a fundamental and totally unparalleled change in our jurisprudence has unlimited possibilities for inflicting confiscatory liabilities upon defendants. We know that statistics can be used to prove anything. One can imagine a price-fixing case in a basic industry. Statistical experts could estimate how much the price of a product was increased due to the violation. They could also extrapolate consequential increases in the price of finished materials, or price increases through each stage of distribution, or increases in the price of housing, automobiles and other end products; and some would not hesitate to attribute to the violation such injuries to the "general economy" as the spiraling of inflationary costs in all products and services. Such monstrous speculative damages could bankrupt the largest firms.

But the issue is really not the little plaintiffs versus the big defendants. Indeed, anyone scanning the list of antitrust cases filed each month will be amazed at the few defendants whose names are familiar. Obviously the most likely losers will be the smaller firms, particularly those inexperienced in antitrust, unable to afford costly litigation, and terribly vulnerable to costly settlements in order to avoid the risk of devastating verdicts.

Of course, it is often said that these global recoveries are the only way to reach a hypothetical defendant who has cheated such a large number of consumers that they could not form a manageable class under existing rules. Frankly, I think this argument is a red herring. How many cases of widespread consumer injury can even be imagined where there are no intervening parties with a substantial enough interest to make private actions practical? What evidence is there that these potential actions by middlemen — or indeed by manageable subclasses of consumers, particularly when we bear in mind existing criminal penalties — are an insufficient deterrent to would-be violators?

I believe that even under existing law the balance weighs so much against the defendant that meritless cases are won or, more likely, settled at heavy cost. The antitrust class action, as one judge said recently, has become "an overwhelmingly costly and potent engine for the compulsion of settlements, whether just or unjust."[11] Surely we who specialize in antitrust should be concerned about justice and fairness. There is also the concern for the burden on the federal court system — antitrust class actions were up 60 percent in 1975 over 1974. But I think our primary concern must be for the impact of this litigation explosion on weakening the free market itself in terms of lessening competition, protecting and creating inefficiency, and increasing cost to the consumer.

Every court decision or jury verdict which protects a plaintiff from competition, as in the cases I have cited, imposes costs and inefficiencies upon the defendant for competing vigorously. Penalty rather than reward follows from doing the best job for the customer. Every settlement of a meritless case — and I am convinced that the unbalanced risks of litigation foster many such settlements — is a misallocation of resources like any other economic inefficiency.

The damage does not stop there. The inevitable result of these escalated risks is a weakening of the vigor of competition and the raising of costs to the consumer. When the risks of losing a suit are so staggering and when the boundary between an antitrust offense and a socially beneficial competitive business practice is so thin, the tendency will be to tilt business decisions away from efficiency and vigorous competitive behavior in favor of reducing the risks. "When in doubt, don't" applies here also.

The efficient company, for example, will ease off on price competition rather than take too much business away from the potential plaintiff-competitor. A manufacturer will tolerate inefficiency in a distributor rather than run the risk of being penalized for putting a more efficient one in his place. And the free market system and the consumer will suffer.

With these results from expanding antitrust remedies and enforcement, we seem to be coming to the point where antitrust enforcement is looked at as an end in itself, instead of being regarded as only a means to achieve the underlying objectives of promoting and preventing interference with a competitive market. Instead of trying to eliminate government-imposed restraints that are the real threat to our economic system, we are in danger of making the hanging of the accused the proof of our dedication to antitrust, even where the effect is to hamper or lessen the vigor of competition.

Men have engaged in such unfortunate and irrational crusades before. In the 12th and 13th centuries the elimination of heresy became a goal in itself. It was assumed that the accused were always guilty and so the innocent were condemned. Material incentives were provided for those who helped to round up the victims. What commenced as a mission to spread a gospel based on love was forgotten and aborted in an emotional zeal for enforcement.

We do not need to accept the comparable rhetoric employed today by those in our society who insist that our competitive system is no good, that we are engulfed in corporate crime, and that the American consumer is systematically cheated. Surely we are mature enough, both in business and in government, to recognize that antitrust does not mean antibusiness. Surely we are capable of reestablishing antitrust enforcement and related economic policies resolutely and solely in the direction of promoting competition.

Legislative efforts should be directed at enabling the marketplace to function by eliminating unnecessary government regulations and monopolies rather than by seeking to establish more and more counterproductive antitrust remedies and penalties. The courts, too, must be vigilant to see that the law is interpreted to promote competition, not to protect competitors from competition. And only the judiciary can ensure that the class-action process, rules of evidence, and trial procedures are not weighted so heavily against the accused that mistakes are induced and vigorous competition transmuted into violations of law.

And finally, it seems to me that the lawyers of the antitrust bar also have an obligation here. Because their practice gives them special experience and understanding of the competitive system, they have a unique capability to inform and educate legislators, judges and the public alike on the proper role of antitrust in fostering the free market.

If all concerned — legislators, judges and lawyers — can keep to the true purposes of antitrust, I think we can have a national antitrust policy that is not anticompetitive, but one which will continue to work positively in behalf of the free market and society.

[1] S. 1, 94th Cong., 1st Sess. §2201 (c)(1975).

[2] Senate Amendment No.396 to S. 1284, 94th Cong., 1st Sess. (1975).

[3] S. 1167, 93rd Cong., 1st Sess. (1973), reintroduced with minor changes as S. 1959, 94th Cong., 1st Sess. (1975). S. 2387, 94th Cong., 1st Sess. (1975); S. 489, 94th Cong., 1st Sess. (1975); S. 2761, 94th Cong., 1st Sess. (1975).

[4] H. R. 8532, 94th Cong., 1st Sess. (1975). S. 1284, 94th Cong., 1st Sess., §401 (1975).

[5] "Antitrust Procedures and Penalties Act," P.L. 93-528, December 21, 1974.

[6] *Free World Foreign Cars, Inc. v. Alfa Romeo*, 55 FRD 26, 30 (S.D.N.Y., 1972).

[7] *Albrecht v. Herald Co.*, 390 U.S. 145 (1968).

[8] *Utah Pie v. Continental Baking Co.*, 386 U.S. 685 (1967).

[9] *Telex Corp. v. International Business Machines Corp.*, 367 F. Supp. 258 (N.D. Okla., 1973), rev'd, 510 F.2d 894 (10th Cir., 1975).

[10] *United States v. General Motors Corp.*, 1974 -2 Trade Cases, CCH TRR, ¶75,253 at 97, 671 (E.D. Mich., 1974).

[11] *Kline v. Coldwell, Banker & Co.*, 508 F.2d 226, 238 (9th Cir., 1974).

Toward a National Antitrust Policy? – 2

Peter O. Steiner

DO WE, as some clearly believe, need major new antitrust legislation? This involves three further questions: (1) Should the goals of antitrust policy be expanded? My answer is no. (2) Are there significant deficiencies in our present policies? My answer is yes. (3) Is new legislation the way to remedy such deficiencies as may exist? My answer is no. I do not mean to suggest that significant changes in policy may not be warranted. I mean instead to suggest that the evolution that is occurring is more promising than the proposals for legislative surgery. (Of course, like each of you, I have my own agenda of ideal legislation that I would be glad to see enacted if only Congress could be trusted to do it my way *and* if the courts would understand how it was to be interpreted.)

The Goals of Antitrust Policy

I take the traditional goal of antitrust policy to be the preservation (some would say restoration) of a competitive private enterprise system. This involves explicit policy because the economists' first insight ("Markets work!") is tempered by their other insight ("Markets fail!"). One form of market failure is the monopoly problem. There is, and was from the start, a competing concern (Bork calls it a deviant theme) that would interpret antitrust as against bigness rather than in favor of competition.[1] This populist view has a cyclical life of its own, with its most recent upsurge during the merger wave of the late 1960's. It has since receded somewhat but the legislative proposals it spawned are still to be found all around. From this vantage point, as distinct from 1968, there seems to be no new, clear or present danger of the creation of an industrial oligarchy, and I would judge the trend (in defining goals for antitrust) to be back toward competition. The repeal of the Miller-Tydings and McGuire Acts is a straw in this wind. While I do not think that the tradition of Brandeis, Black, Douglas and Patman will ever wholly disappear, it seems in a no-growth phase at the moment.

The traditional goal for antitrust of preserving competition is, in my view, not only still appropriate but quite sufficient. Many other real problems of our society demand attention and some would have us use the antitrust laws to meet them. There are, for example, the many recent examples of corporate, union and governmental abuse of power. But to turn antitrust enforcement to those abuses would not only divert scarce resources, but would decrease the ability to maintain competition by warping the view of what activities merit close surveillance. I remember still the well-intentioned but bizarre suggestion made in 1968 by the Mitchell-Kleindienst-McLaren team to use the antitrust laws as a major weapon in their planned war against organized crime.[2] Fortunately they were dissuaded.

Another suggestion, which should be resisted as well, is to conceive of anti-trust as a major weapon against inflation. While some current antitrust activities, such as attacks on entry restriction in the regulated industries, may have a one-time effect on the *level* of prices in some areas, they have virtually no bearing on the root causes of the *rate of increase of prices* that is inflation.[3] The current inflation is occurring in all sectors of the economy, independent of the vigor of competition. If this seems a straw man, observe how quickly most discussions of the "industrial reorganization" proposals get entwined with the current inflation. If oligopoly power indeed deserves attention, it does so on its own merits, not because of the failures (and there are many) of our macro-economic policies.

Alleged Deficiencies

Proposed legislation is a response to perceived inadequacies in the existing policy arsenal. Let me comment briefly on five areas of alleged deficiency: (1) oligopoly, (2) mergers, (3) pockets of exempt behavior, (4) execrable unilateral conduct, (5) treble damages and other penalties.

Oligopoly

The courts have stubbornly resisted repeated urging to extend to oligopoly "shared monopoly power" — the strict standard of monopolization applied under Section 2 of the Sherman Act. Those who saw the *Aluminum*,[4] *Tobacco*,[5] and *Triangle Conduit*[6] decisions as presaging a "New Sherman Act" before which oligopoly would crumble, were to be disappointed. This disappointment had led to repeated proposals for a large amount of new legislation creating a rebuttable presumption for deconcentration of highly concentrated industry structures. Oligopolistic industries exhibit, par excellence, the competing tensions between the economies of scale in production and distribution that make large enterprises efficient, and the centers of private power that make them capable of abusing the social good. But these tensions have existed from the start and are precisely the ones that make antitrust policy both difficult and important. There is no credible evidence to suggest that the oligopoly problem has recently become more acute. Nor has the structuralist view that high concentration leads with decisively high probability to adverse performance won new logical or empirical support.

Professor James Rahl, writing in 1962, concluded that "there is no consensus of scientific, scholarly, legislative, executive, or judicial opinion in this country as to the wisdom of doing anything very basic about" the oligopoly problem, and nothing since 1962 would lead me to modify his conclusion.[7] Indeed, the current revival of the debate is in response to a challenge from the other side: Professor Yale Brozen's attack on the validity of the association, as a long-run phenomenon, between high concentration ratios and persistent high profits.[8] One does not need to take sides in that debate to read in it a warning against restructuring legislation in this area. We should legislate from knowledge, not from frustration with our ignorance. It may well be that we shall one day know enough to justify a Hart-like industrial reorganization bill or a vertical dismemberment of the oil industry, but I do not believe that that day has yet come.

Mergers

In the years since 1950, when mergers came under effective antitrust control, the courts have adopted very different standards of the amount of market power required to trigger a structural antitrust violation. The policy is most severe on mergers, less severe on market occupancy by a single firm, and least severe on shared power. Few would quarrel with that ordering. The current support for a merger notification bill may reflect a desire for an even more restrictive policy toward mergers. It may, on the other hand, reflect fear that the current Supreme Court will sharply retreat from the position of the Warren Court. At the very least it suggests a recognition that the Merger Guidelines, which promised to become merger policy with a Supreme Court before which "the government always won," are on their way to becoming historical curiosities.

How should one evaluate the proposal? Since the large merger, like the large corporation, is not unambiguously undesirable, a policy proposal that adds to the inhibitions ought to bear the burden of showing that the mergers it will stop ought to be stopped. Giving the Justice Department the power automatically to enjoin large mergers preliminarily (and thus frequently to block them permanently) supposes either a clear need to move the judicially determined line of what is illegal, or to trust the economic judgments of the Department of Justice more than those of the courts. The second supposition seems doubtful on its merits, and doubly so because of the mixing of prosecutorial and judicial functions. As to whether we are now too permissive, I am aware of no evidence that suggests a more restrictive policy is required, or that absolute size (not market share) is the relevant measure. The conglomerate problem, which might have occasioned such legislative concerns in 1968, no longer does — both because of the decline of the phenomenon and, more basically, because the courts have found a way to embrace the problem using potential competition as a sound but flexible standard for integrating conglomerate diversification into the main corpus of antitrust: the effect on competition.

Exemptions

Once we get beyond the exemption of labor unions (and some would challenge even that), virtually every area of actual or de facto exempt behavior has been subject to debate and proposed legislative challenge. The most important exempt areas are the regulated industries. The presumption underlying Section 11 of the Clayton Act was that competitive concerns with respect to the industries they regulate should be delegated to the ICC, the FCC, the CAB, and the FRB. The implicit faith was that regulators, as they acquired knowledge of their industries' problems, would not lose the resolve to achieve the benefits of competition. That faith has been known to be misdirected for at least a generation. Here, quite in contrast to the oligopoly and merger areas, there *is* today a "scientific and scholarly consensus" that increased reliance on competition in regulated industries is in order.

Execrable Unilateral Conduct

Unilateral predatory conduct by one lacking the market power to be charged under Section 2 of the Sherman Act and lacking the multiparty conduct to fall within Section 1, is (arguably) a lacuna in present antitrust coverage.[9] It is not clear to me that there are major adverse competitive consequences in such conduct, but it creates a legal unease, and has invited legislative proposals to close the gap that may have adverse economic consequences. Of course there is always Section 5 of the FTC Act, but that is small comfort to the private victim who seeks either injunctive relief or damages.

Penalties

My interest in the size and nature of penalties is their effect on motivation. It is often argued that the fines assessable in criminal cases are still ludicrously small when assessed against large corporations. If such fines were the only penalties, they would indeed be a primary deficiency of our present laws. But to discuss the disincentive effects of an antitrust prosecution intelligently it is necessary to treat the whole penalty package as one: the criminal penalties to individuals, the fines, the staggering costs of litigation, and the damages (single or treble) in civil suits.

I sense a rising unease about the potential for perverse incentive effects of mandatory treble damages, particularly when piggybacked on class-action suits. Treble damages were initially intended to provide a "finder's fee" to injured plaintiffs and thus to motivate the rooting out of violations that might otherwise escape the eye or budget of the public prosecutor. Even when that economically sound objective was not served because private suits increasingly came in the train of public suits, treble damages could be argued to add desirably to the penalties for violation, and thus both to compensate for generally inadequate deterrents in public suit penalties, and to create a largely laudable incentive for consent decrees or nolo pleas in the kinds of cases that it is desirable to have settled quickly.

Does a different motivation — one closer to extortion, without economic or moral justification — now come into play? After issuance of a complaint in a governmental suit, a flood of class-action, treble-damage suits is all but automatic, and can be initiated at relatively little cost. These cases, in turn, are likely to be collected in a single court for trial, thus all but assuring they will all be decided the same way. A defendant determined to fight the public case on its merits may expose himself to enormous risk if he should lose. Suppose, to see the issue clearly, a seller of a commodity with unit value of $100 sold one million units per year over 10 years. If a jury ultimately (albeit wrongly) finds damages of $10 per unit over the entire period, the seller faces a $300 million penalty (plus attorneys' fees). For a company with sales of $100 million per year this is surely an awesome prospect. Suppose its activities were in fact legal, and it did not wish to accept a consent decree. Suppose there is still one chance in 100 that it will lose both public and private suits. (Is there ever less chance than that?) The "expected value" of his loss is more than $3 million but the loss, if it occurs, will be ruinous.[10] Is the seller not safer to settle the private suits before they really begin, for say $2 million (or even $4 million)? It is a risk-prone lawyer who advises his client otherwise. Yet such thinking invites suits whose only purpose is such a settlement. Defendants collectively should share the risks and fight such suits, but acting independently the risk is too great.

14

If, as I believe, remedies and penalties are a problem area, it is because the "package" has developed without plan and without comprehensive review as inflation, tax rates, tax rulings, ease of getting standing for private suits, ease of maintaining class actions, etc., have changed. Moreover what is illegal keeps changing in unforeseen ways. It would be remarkable if the present penalty package were optimal, and there is lots of reason to suppose it is not.

Is Legislation Required?

Even in my relatively sanguine review, there are identified deficiencies in three areas: unwise exemptions, unilateral predatory conduct, and damages and penalties considered broadly. Are these prime candidates for legislative reform? I think not.

The whole history of antitrust in this country gives pause against heavy reliance on the statutory remedy. As a statutory field, antitrust invites statutory reform. But the basic statute was constitutionlike in its language and provided the invitation — if not the necessity — to the judiciary to develop a common law of antitrust. Such judicial interpretation has frequently led to dissatisfaction and to subsequent legislative reform. But the corrective legislation seldom promptly accomplished what it intended and it often invited adverse adaptive responses.

Both the FTC Act and the Clayton Act were legislative responses to the first two decades of the Sherman Act — each was intended to correct deficiencies that by 1914 bothered either the populists or the business community, or both. Hardly any feature of either Act worked as intended. Neither the creation of the FTC as a specialized agency which, with professional expertise, was expected to fashion a sensible law of restraints of trade, nor the incredibly detailed language of Sections 2 and 3 of the Clayton Act, succeeded in taking discretion from the federal courts nor created the certainty that business wanted. Neither Act resolved the latent conflict between preservation of competition and protection of small competitors. The original Section 7, attempting to meet a demonstrated failure to cope with the merger problem, probably did more damage than good by inducing asset acquisitions in place of the prohibited stock acquisitions. It was to be 36 years before a sound antimerger statute was enacted. This Celler-Kefauver Act — surely the triumph of the post-Sherman Act legislative history — succeeded because it was legislation based upon knowledge, not ignorance; upon recognized deficiencies, not vague unease. There ought to be a lesson in that. As to the other major legislative attempts, Webb-Pomerene, Miller-Tydings, McGuire and Robinson-Patman, the less said the better. They surely do not make legislation (other than repeal) seem promising.

If detailed legislative reform has been one of the unhappy experiences in antitrust, judicial abdication has been the other. Both in the early 1920's, when the spirit was "anything goes," and in the mid-1960's when everything went, delegation of the defense of competition either to private conscience or to the Justice Department's prosecutorial discretion seems to me to have been unsatisfactory.

Notwithstanding everyone's ability to conjure up a collection of horrors in Supreme Court decision making, it has been judicial construction and evolution that (with Sections 1 and 2 of the Sherman Act and the revised Section 7 of the Clayton Act) have developed and continue to develop a national antitrust policy. In broad outline this policy is both effective and sensible, and has shown a remarkable ability to evolve and to adapt to changes in both political mood and whatever scholarly consensus exists.

We forget, I think, that antitrust is younger than its years. In terms of a period of sustained interest and attention, it really dates only from the end of World War II. Of course many of the cases decided in the early ·postwar years were commenced in the period following Thurman Arnold's coming to the Antitrust Division in 1937. But the World War II interruption was an important one.

Before then, we had no sustained period with both executive willingness to push it, and judicial willingness to explore the outer boundaries; since then, there have been no periods of hiatus. In virtually every area except simple price fixing, antitrust policy has come a long way since 1945. (Indeed in some areas it has, in my view, come too far, but there I have little doubt that a more nearly balanced court can find its way back.)

While all of this leads me to a presumption against a legislative reform if a judicial response is possible, the presumption is of course rebuttable. Legislation has worked well where there is a well-defined need; where there is a consensus as to how to proceed; and where the possibilities of unsatisfactory side effects seem small. Thus the Celler-Kefauver Act seemed a happier response to the merger problem than a stretching or twisting of Section 1 of the Sherman Act. With respect to the principal current deficiency areas, I am not presently persuaded.

(1) The erosion of areas of de facto exempt behavior is progressing constructively without new legislation. *Goldfarb* has opened the possibility of bringing professional services generally into a single antitrust policy;[11] the doubtful special treatment of professional sports seems unlikely to survive for long; most important, the fringes of regulation are being opened up to doses of entry and competition, and a more massive rethinking of regulatory policy is under way. While that rethinking may in due course entail new legislation, at the moment conventional avenues of reform seem to be effective. Indeed the Justice Department's AT&T suit seems at least as much an attack on past regulatory decisions as on any of "Ma Bell's" activities.[12]

(2) While a new statute could deal with unilateral predatory conduct by defining unfair competition as a crime open to private plaintiffs, I doubt if it could be limited to socially undesirable practices. My fear is that such a statute, like Robinson-Patman, would tend to shield competitors at the expense of competition more often than it would be procompetitive. The stubborn vitality of the Robinson-Patman Act, despite the all but unanimous view of disinterested observers that it is an anticompetitive statute, is not reassuring. The small businessman, the harassed distributor, and the generally unagressive competitor are too numerous to make the legislative arena a promising source of reform. I think the dangers of bad legislation are sufficiently large here, that it is, if necessary, preferable to live with the problem. Of course, the unilateral execrable conduct lacuna (if it is that) can be reached without new legislation, though at the expense of keeping the Section 2 of the Sherman Act "attempts" standard

fuzzy. Such behavior could be embraced by the courts' further eroding the quantum of power that constitutes monopoly (thus bringing ever closer the thing of which there is a dangerous probability) or by following Professor Turner's suggestion of accepting a trade-off between power and conduct such that, in the face of foul conduct without redeeming value, one forgets to look further for power.[13] While there is much to be said against a fuzzy standard, such as now governs Section 2 attempts cases, there is something to be said for it if the alternative is bad enough, and the need is great enough.

(3) Finally we come to penalties. My problem here is that I have no sense that a coherent consensus exists of what to do, and that is a dangerous posture from which to draft legislation. The need for a coordinated view of both private and public penalties seems crucial, yet difficult to manage, and none of the current legislative proposals attempts one. To neglect such coordination is to neglect the evident fact that the private suit and the public one go hand in glove, and that the private penalties provide the major deterrents. Is the schedule of penalties provided in current legislation sensible? Surely it depends on how the courts expand or contract the private suit. Here, again, evolution seems to be at work. If *Bigelow*[14] opened up the private suit at the beginning of the modern era, *Eisen*[15] may have started to limit its potential for becoming the tail that wags the dog.

Let me come finally to the title question. In my view we *have* a vital and evolving national antitrust policy. It seems certain, no matter which party controls the government, that we will continue to have an Antitrust Division that enforces this policy and attempts to change its limits, and a Judiciary that shapes it to the world it sees. The more striking current proposals for legislative reform seem to me dictated more by ideology than by evidence of malfunction, and by broader concerns about the nature of our society than can sensibly be implemented through an antitrust policy.

[1] Robert Bork, "The Rule of Reason and the Per Se Concept" I 75 *Yale Law Journal* 775 (April, 1965).

[2] This was made to the Task Force on Productivity and Competition (Stigler Task Force) appointed by President-elect Nixon to advise him on antitrust matters, of which I was a member.

[3] To lower prices by (say) 5 percent would lead to an apparent reduction in the inflation in the year in which it occurred. But those (lower) prices would increase in each subsequent year if the general inflation continued.

[4] *United States v. Aluminum Co. of America*, 148 F. 2d 416 (1945).

[5] *American Tobacco Co. v. United States*, 328 U.S. 781 (1946).

[6] *Triangle Conduit & Cable Co. v. Federal Trade Commission*, 168 F. 2d 175 (7th Cir., 1948).

[7] James Rahl, "Price Competition and the Price Fixing Rule" 57 *Northwestern University Law Review* 137 (1962).

[8] Yale Brozen, "The Antitrust Task Force Deconcentration Recommendation" 13 *Journal of Law & Economics* 270 (1970). See also 14 *J.L.E.* 493-512 (1971).

[9] See generally Edward H. Cooper, "Attempts and Monopolization: A Mildly Expansionary Answer to the Prophylactic Riddle of Section 2" 72 *Michigan Law Review* 373 (1974).

[10] The expected value is the product of the value, if it occurs, times the probability of occurrence.

[11] *Goldfarb v. Virginia State Bar,* 95 S. Ct 2004.

[12] See the complaint *United States v. American Telephone and Telegraph Co.* CA 74-1698 D.D.C. (Nov. 1974) in *Antitrust & Trade Regulation Report* No. 690 (Nov. 26, 1974) pp. D1-D4.

[13] Turner suggested this as early as 1956. See Donald Turner, "Antitrust Policy and the Cellophane Case" 70 *Harvard Law Review* 281 at 305 (1956).

[14] *Bigelow v. RKO Radio Pictures Inc.,* 327 U.S. 251 (1946).

[15] *Eisen v. Carlisle & Jacquelin,* 417 U.S. 156 (1974).

Dialogue on

Information Problems and Antitrust

Frederick M. Rowe, Moderator
Kenneth W. Dam • *Ira M. Millstein* • *Howard L. Siers*

•

MR. FREDERICK M. ROWE: Information Problems and Antitrust, our luncheon topic today, is an area rife with controversy, litigation and confusion. As government intervention and regulation proliferate, the big subpoena and the fat questionnaire symbolize the public quest for business data as a basis for economic policy decisions. Such government inquests not only cast heavy burdens of compliance on business firms, but raise vexing issues of cost benefit, garbles between static regulatory concepts and dynamic business actualities, paradoxes of disclosures which may inhibit competition, and overarching issues as to utility, relevance and significance of facts in the eyes of the beholder.

Thus, Line of Business I begets Line of Business II. Corporate Patterns is born as the "son" of Line of Business. The issues are polarized by lawyers, courts and preliminary injunctions. A Federal Paperwork Commission seeks to cut multibillion dollar cost burdens on the economy, and to move the immovable bureaucratic mountains. The looming specter of central economic planning foreshadows more information needs and more pressures toward data standardization to fit preconceived regulatory concepts legitimized by an asserted public right to know.

Are we then fated to wallow in an information orgy? Or are there some parameters for policy guidance as to what business information is or is not appropriate for disclosure to government or to others? And without such parameters, who will pay the price?

These topics and others will be addressed by our distinguished panel consisting today of Professor Kenneth W. Dam, of the University of Chicago Law School; Ira M. Millstein, a prominent leader of the antitrust profession; and Howard L. Siers, Assistant Comptroller of E.I. du Pont de Nemours & Company, who is responsible for Du Pont's accounting systems and procedures.[1]

I would like to begin our dialogue with this question of broad general interest: In view of the prevalent assumption that the provision of information by business firms to government and to the public is a good thing, in an absolute sense, is there something peculiar about information in this respect? Is there an information mystique?

MR. KENNETH W. DAM: Well, my answer would be "yes" and "no." It's certainly true that the public, the Congress, and many in the rest of the government view information as something special. In fact, they often seem to view it as a free good. But following University of Chicago economic teachings, I think we all know by now that there is no such thing as a free lunch. Obviously, in dealing with public policy issues involving information, one has to measure costs against benefits, and when one does that, the analysis is very similar to any good. But there is one respect in which information is special. Once information has been produced for one person, the marginal cost of producing it for others is either zero or approaches zero.

MR. IRA M. MILLSTEIN: I think that nicely frames the problem facing us in the information area. We have to divide information into two groups: (1) that which exists and (2) that which does not exist. I believe both groups are sought. In one situation, it has been argued by some, the cost-benefit ratio approaches zero — namely, the information exists, and you really do not have to spend a lot of money to get it out. I'd like to talk about that just for a minute, because accounting data are not the whole story about information. There is a great deal of other information that is sought and that we have to take account of.

Perhaps it's best crystallized in the recent report by the Corporate Accountability Research Group — a Nader organization — in *The Case for the Federal Chartering of Giant Corporations.*[2] If you want to see the kinds of information the disclosure of which is being urged, you should take a spin through this report. I made a quick list. The Nader people would like corporate disclosure of investment interests in other companies; other kinds of affiliations, including long-term contracts and joint ventures; information about suppliers, customers, patents and know-how license agreements; government funding for R and D; government defense procurement payments; federal loans and grants; tax information; information as to large stockholders; management compensation (monetary and otherwise, including chauffeur driven cars); information on pollution caused by manufacturing plants — what wastes are discharged, how deadly are they — the details about compliance with EPA requirements; information on occupational health and safety; minority employment; advertising and lobbying activities — among other things.[3]

As to such information, it has been argued by some, you can apply no real cost-benefit analysis because the information exists. As for the other set of information, however — namely, accounting and other data which do not exist and have to be generated — there you are better able to use cost-benefit analysis.

MR. ROWE: Howard, doesn't Du Pont have all that?

MR. HOWARD L. SIERS: Well, let me first say that business information is a very broad subject. It is not just accounting and financial data. We're talking about a number of the items that Ira has mentioned here, environmental protection, pollution control, EEO, ERISA — you know them as well as I do. Sure, we have most of the information. I don't think any company would deny that it has such detailed data. After all, it does exist or can be developed from a company's most elementary records. As an example, we could replicate our entire file — everything we have in our records if that's what it takes, every invoice, every bill of lading, every payroll record. You name it, we'll have it.

Then we could have an "open house" and everybody could come in and could pick and choose; use only the wanted information and arrive at the wanted conclusions. A kind of "do-it-yourself data kit." I've also had people respond by saying, "Let's just back a truck up and load it up and let them sort it out." After all, that's the way we have to compile data. But let's be serious for a moment and recognize that you're always faced with understanding and interpreting the data — not just collecting and reporting them.

In the first place, the data are recorded by a lot of people in a lot of different locations. They have to be organized, processed, analyzed and researched. They have to be interpreted and explained to various levels of management. All of that's an internal process. Then, having done that, we share this information with our shareholders, with all kinds of government agencies and various parts of the public. And I think you have to recognize that if this information is to be of value, it must be properly interpreted. There is a major cost associated with it and there must be a related benefit.

MR. ROWE: Howard, you talked about "open house" at Wilmington, and that this is a massive information job. But with big corporations in the public eye today, and the rising clamor about concentration of power, corporate secrecy, and corporate morality, does the social benefit of disclosure by corporations of great size possibly outweigh the burdens and the cost of generating the data?

MR. MILLSTEIN: Well, Fred, I think at least two things are happening. The first is a trend — a trend following Watergate and Vietnam, the CIA and foreign arrangements; namely, pure sunshine. Everyone has to know everything about everything. There's no sense fooling ourselves. It's here; it's a fact; people do feel that way whether it's rational or not. Put that to one side. It's just a fact of life with which we have to deal.

Second, there is an increasing tendency to view the corporation as having a public aspect. Some people are beginning to view the corporation as an entity which is subject to a variety of pressures and tensions; and the argument is that performance gets better if the corporation has to respond to these different tensions. Who provides the tensions?

Consumers provide a tension. They make demands for quality, price and service. Stockholders provide a tension, as do the banks, which put up the capital and make certain demands for adequate returns. Employees are a tension-creating mechanism. They seek adequate compensation and security in employment as well as in retirement. Competitors provide a tension. Alert to weaknesses, they compel efficiency in the corporation. The government provides a further tension as the umpire, the policeman, who is always watching to assure that all these varying constituencies are somehow or other satisified.

What's information got to do with that? Well, the school of thought is that information is the fuel which gives each one of these constituencies the ability to place the tension on the corporation to which it should respond; that better performance will result from the corporate effort to vector a course which attempts to respond to intelligent tension. I think that's what a fair number of people think about corporations today, and it's something which requires dealing with.

MR. ROWE: Doesn't "sunshine" and the need to satisfy these tensions in our society make the case for broad disclosure and for open house at Wilmington and elsewhere?

MR. DAM: I don't have any real problems with what I shall call the Millstein "interest-group theory" of the corporation, provided we take it simply as an objective statement of what is happening. But I have serious problems about the implications of what is happening. It seems to me that we should look at the costs not merely of providing the information that is demanded but also the potential costs to the society — to all of us — of the change in behavior of corporations resulting from this new interest-group environment. What we should be interested in when looking at the economy as a whole is how corporations will respond to these nonmarket pressures. Will they respond in a way that benefits all of us? Will companies continue to make the risky investment, especially one that produces losses for several years, if they know that it's going to be disclosed immediately. Will they seek a less expensive labor force if they must disclose that they're going to do so before they even start looking? Will they move to a cheaper plant in another part of the country? If not, then the effect of this interest-group theory that is evolving will be pernicious.

MR. MILLSTEIN: Well, this is always the problem with the Chicago school. You take it to the extreme because where you leave me is, "Leave us alone." "I'll tell you nothing because if I tell you everything, it will be terrible." Now, I question whether it's that extreme.

MR. ROWE: We have heard about sunshine and clouds in Chicago, but is this all at the expense of the open house?

MR. SIERS: I'd like to address that question. We're talking about the need for this information and we have our ideal world, and everybody is going to get this information and do something about it. My question is, how much is all of this ideal information worth? Because every time you put a new information burden or demand on a company, there's a cost in developing the information, understanding and distributing it, and, once having distributed it, explaining it. I guess the classic answer any time you raise the specter of cost of information is always "recover it in your profits." Higher selling prices, higher profits. But I submit that there's a limit to what kind of price increases this economy can sustain and continue to have any growth. At some point, the cost burden of doing all of these ideal information-gathering operations will cause us to raise our selling prices to such an extent that it will drive us out of the marketplace.

And all of this is in the shadow of one of the major problems facing industry today, actually facing the entire economy. And that's the great difficulty that we all foresee in providing the near-term and longer-term capital formation needs of our economy. To the extent that you spend a dollar to develop unnecessary information, this is a dollar spent on nonproductive costs that could better be invested in productive facilities that will help to benefit our economy in the future.

MR. ROWE: Apparently, sunshine doesn't come for free; it has costs.

But let's come off the clouds and the sunshine to the mundane problem of our agenda today: Information and Antitrust. I'd like to start by asking, why is antitrust so notorious for huge and burdensome data creation in litigation as well as in antitrust policymaking?

MR. MILLSTEIN: Let me kick that one off. Antitrust lawyers are by nature packrats. They live on information; they thrive on it. Without information a case can't be tried. There's a serious reason for this in antitrust matters, because more than law is involved; while there's obviously a legal judgment involved, there's also an economic judgment involved.

Everybody is trying to convince the court that the conduct involved is somehow justified or unjustified from an economic standpoint. Given that, all of the circumstances surrounding the conduct in question become relevant. The market, the industry, its growth, the individual firms, competitors, customers, suppliers, the product, its prices, R and D, costs, motivation, intent — it's all on "paper," in depositions, in reference materials, and elsewhere. These are just examples. Anything that has to do with the company, the individuals involved, the industry, gives you a crack at drawing a favorable or unfavorable inference about the conduct; and it all depends on which hat you're wearing. So information is critical. Indeed, antitrust lawyers are monuments to overkill in information. We put economists and accountants to work with regressions and the like, and we get these huge printouts that we either put in drawers and save or bring to court for the court to look at and, frequently, refuse to accept in evidence.

MR. DAM: But note, Ira, that here it's not the enforcement authorities, or even the self-appointed representatives of the public interest, that are requiring disclosure. It's the companies themselves that are engaging in this information-gathering process. First of all, there are the defense lawyers who want to understand their case fully. More particularly, it is the defendants who typically have been trying to provide more information to the court than the court has wanted to accept. That's the basic reason for the growth of judge-made *per se* rules, which render a lot of this information irrelevant and, therefore, dispensable.

MR. MILLSTEIN: Well, I have to say there appears to be a little irony in the fact that a defendant will spend millions for defense but not one cent for tribute; namely, generating the data that allegedly are required for public-policy purposes. There is an irony involved, assuming that the information sought is demonstrably needed and usable for public-policy purposes.

MR. ROWE: How about it, Howard? You pay millions for defense and also for tribute.

MR. SIERS: I think that you have two different situations here. To provide data routinely on a "just in case somebody wants it" basis would be extremely expensive and very difficult to organize because we just don't have a crystal ball that lets us know what everybody wants to know. On the other hand, we do have certain needs for routine information and we do collect this information. When we're faced with a problem in marshalling the truckloads of information for our antitrust situations, generally speaking, our response is to organize a task force. We completely disrupt our organization and we assign whatever manpower it takes fulltime to get that job accomplished. I submit that if we were to have to establish a task force to address itself to every problem or every competitive move that came down the pike to understand whether or not we should respond to the same degree that we do to pull this information together for antitrust purposes, that would become our primary business. We wouldn't be in the business of making chemicals and fibers, we'd be in the business of producing data and there is a bottom-line requirement for all of this.

Any time you pull information together for antitrust purposes, every bit of that information, as I'm sure all of you are aware, goes under the microscope. I think it just goes without saying anything more that we just couldn't afford to absorb that kind of cost in industry. We respond to a very specific situation in an antitrust case. We know what the questions are. We can develop the answers. On the other hand, to provide data for something that somebody might ask out in the future is beyond our capability.

MR. ROWE: The question is, do we know the question?

MR. DAM: I believe that it's a bit more complicated than Ira suggested on the benefit side, not just on the cost side, because even in an antitrust case, one knows very specifically what the question is. But it's not so clear what the question will turn out to be in the more general public-policy arena. Take a question involving prices. You may have every one of your invoices. When you have an antitrust case, you will know how you want to process all that information. But suppose you're just asked to make the information generally available.

Are we interested in the price? Are we interested in quantity? Are we interested in the discounts, or in price in one area versus price in another, or price by kind of customer, or price changes over time? Obviously, we can't be sure in advance. Since we don't know what the question will turn out to be, I'm not sure that the information can intelligently be put together in a form that is both understandable and not inherently misleading, no matter how great the cost.

MR. MILLSTEIN: I think what Ken is putting his finger on is that our discussion is beginning to move away from what information is needed to defend an antitrust case, to the matter of the information needed and relevant to policy planning. And the problem which Ken is pointing out is that we don't know the kinds of information needed for and relevant to policy planning. However, I do think we are beginning to learn some of the questions which are being asked for policy-planning purposes, and I think one of the most irritating and difficult is the whole question of segment reporting.

I think we know that some policy planners in the antitrust area are looking at profits, R and D, and advertising on a segment basis. That's what they're looking for and it seems to me that it's going to take a lot of dollars and a lot of effort to get at it, *if* it can be gotten at. But passing that for the minute, the next element is, what do they want it for? This is what's troubling everybody. I think if all they did was say they wanted it to do a little thinking, to mush around with it, nobody would get terribly excited.

However, they don't know, we don't know what they want it for, and I think that's the irritating aspect of this. Sometimes I wonder if these particular policy planners would not be better advised to decide what they wanted it for before they started asking for it. Maybe industry ought to be given the answers to the second question before they have to go to all the manifold burdens of answering the first.

MR. ROWE: We have remarked before on these social pressures. We have also observed the huge sums that are expended in defense of antitrust litigations. IBM is an example. Let's assume the planners do want to go mushing around. Why could not corporations satisfy these mushing-around needs, and get the monkey off their backs?

MR. SIERS: There are several aspects to that question that I would like to cover. First, let's start out by recognizing that the basic source of all business data is the individual company. That's where it has to start. The basic financial transaction; the basic business decision. It starts with the individual company. That's where we start to pull it together.

Under our system, which I think is a good one, every company is free to organize internally as it sees fit, as it interprets its need in the marketplace. So obviously it's going to organize primarily along the lines of whatever its current management philosophy is. In like respect, I think organization is dynamic. As management changes, or even management ideas change, then organization has to change. We can quickly think in terms of the various ways in which companies organize.

Some companies organize to be managed centrally; others have a very decentralized organization. Some companies are organized vertically. Others horizontally. Other companies operate as cost centers; some as profit centers. And there is a significant difference in the way you structure your information system. Also, in approaching this question, you ought to distinguish between total company information and segment information. A segment of an individual company (and I think Ira has properly stated our concern here) is not with regard to total company information, but with regard to information about a portion of individual companies. I think that when we address ourselves to the internal information systems of a company, we have to expect that the information system will be tailored to support its organization, because the management wants to know about its business on the basis on which it is organized.

Given the fact that we are free to organize as we see fit and every individual company will organize in that manner, we therefore have about as many organizations or different types of organizations as we have managers. You're going to have a variety of organizations and a variety of information systems. I think that as a result of these different informational systems, you'll find much more concern in a company that is organized with considerable emphasis on a profit-center management approach than in one that is not.

In like respect, a company such as mine would have much greater emphasis on cost systems that are designed to support continuous process operations, whereas a company that is involved in assembling major items of equipment might be more interested in a job-order cost system. So the cost systems are different. Of course, that again has a major impact on your information system.

I'd like to summarize by saying that there is no "cookbook" approach as to how any one company organizes or even as to how the companies within an industry organize. It always comes back to how the management of an individual company want to organize its business.

Let's move to the fact that two or more companies may have the same basic information system. Then they have opportunities to select among various accounting conventions. They can use straight-line depreciation or accelerated depreciation. We can value our inventories on LIFO or FIFO — and you get tremendous differences in reported results. You could get differences of a magnitude of as much as two-to-one in the profit area alone if you are on LIFO as against FIFO. Because one company selects a given information system or a given accounting convention rather than another, it does not mean that any company's selection is wrong. That company has selected that particular system because it thinks it is the most appropriate system for its management to use in measuring the results of its business. What I'm saying here is that the system is pertinent and appropriate to each individual company.[4]

There are also a couple of myths that I'd like to expand on a bit. Critics frequently observe that we have to know certain information in order to manage our business. For example, you have to know the revenue, cost and investment for each product. I submit that it depends on the level of detail — whether you're talking of product-group cost detail or whether you're talking of individual product detail, as to whether or not a company may or may not routinely have such information.

I think a well-organized company will collect the minimum necessary information in order to inform its management on a routine basis. You will then be prepared to operate on a special study basis to develop details of cost or revenue on a finer breakdown of products or different measurements of performance in the marketplace. One of the real problems we have is that each of us in our own companies probably has a different view of just what markets we are in. And whereas we might think in terms of a given group of products as being one market, another company might feel that it was straddling two markets in those same product lines. So when you pull this information together, and you're looking differently at markets, you start out with a built-in difference in the view of the individual company or companies.

The second item I want to talk about briefly here is the fact that the other criticism we get deals with unlimited information via computers. All you do is press a button and you can get any information you want. And I think that many people believe there's one corporate computer. It's in this one room and that's all we have to worry about. The truth of the matter is, and here I have to speak only from my own experience but I think that this can be reasonably applied to industry in general, I know our computer information system is a network of computers that straddles several generations of computer technology and involves a number of different programming languages. In some instances these computers don't or can't speak to each other.

If we want to get one computer to speak to another, we frequently have to transcribe the information from that system to another manually. With this technology available, people ask why don't you do something about it? It's very simple. Everything we do in the computer field has to have a cost-benefit relationship. I'd love to have a large corporate computer to give me all the answers, but I haven't been able to develop a cost-benefit relationship yet, and that's what it takes if we're going to have these massive data banks that give us all of this information at little or no marginal cost.[5]

Those are the things that I feel are necessary to understand when we are addressing ourselves to differences among individual companies. The information that a company develops is pertinent as long as it's properly interpreted and understood by the management of that company, but when you try to compare one company with the other, this is where I think you run into real problems.

MR. ROWE: What I understand you to say, Howard, and I think you stated it very convincingly, is that these requests for information on an across-the-board breakdown basis don't really jibe with the way a company such as yours generates information for its own internal purposes.

Are there any other comments by the panelists as to why information on the individualized basis that Howard has described should or should not be disclosed by corporations?

MR. DAM: There's one point that I'm curious about. Assume the disclosure of transaction prices is made either directly or indirectly to the public on a current basis. I've always been curious about the fact that if the companies had chosen to exchange that information among themselves, they would be running a substantial antitrust risk. I think that fact reflects the notion that the exchange of information with respect to prices and quantities can lead to a *de facto* situation akin to price fixing.

Does it really make any difference if the public and purchasers also obtain this information? I'm not so sure. Now there is a European idea that "transparency" of the market is extremely important, that everyone — buyers and sellers alike — ought to know everything and, that if they did, that would reduce uncertainty and produce a perfect market. But that transparency concept hasn't been part of the traditional U.S. antitrust philosophy.

MR. MILLSTEIN: There is a body of thought — with which I do not agree — that large companies in concentrated industries ought not to give out information publicly, even if done unilaterally, forgetting about agreements, trade associations, or anything of the sort. It is asserted to be a bad thing for a large company to make information public. Why? Well, the allegation is that if a corporation makes disclosure of prices or costs or whatever, it may lead to some forms of uniformity evoking conceptual problems.

I object to that theory and don't think it's right. However, whether one accepts this notion or not, it's paradoxical that the very information — the disclosure of which may be compelled by the government — might under some theories be objected to. I don't know that this problem has been thought through from a competitive standpoint. It appears paradoxical: On the one hand greater disclosure; on the other hand possible conceptual problems from disclosure.

MR. DAM: I think that you have identified an important issue. I can understand disclosure for other purposes, following your interest-group theory perhaps. But from a strictly competitive point of view, I think it is an open question as to which approach best furthers competition.

MR. MILLSTEIN: From a competitive standpoint, I haven't seen very much yet that really comes to grips with that. I don't know whether this has been your experience but it has been mine: Some important aspects of disclosure remain unanswered in competitive philosophy.

MR. ROWE: Are you saying that it doesn't make any difference whether the disclosure is privately given by one corporation to another corporation, or whether it is made public by a third party for all corporations?

MR. MILLSTEIN: What difference does it make? Once the competitor has the information — whether it's obtained by industrial espionage or publication by the FTC — he has the information. And I think the issue is not how the information was obtained. But assuming no conspiracy, what difference does it make, really? You have the information, and I don't think that the economists and antitrust philosophers have sufficiently grappled with the issue of whether or not such lawful total and open information disclosure in the marketplace really is a good thing or a bad thing competively.

MR. ROWE: It's a very interesting side effect, because in essence what the government would be doing is what trade associations in past years have been penalized and chastized for from an antitrust standpoint.

MR. MILLSTEIN: It's a problem, and it's one I think the planners ought to consider. Maybe they ought to give companies absolution. Anybody who complies with the line-of-business or CPR program is automatically absolved of any antitrust charges.

MR. ROWE: I think we'd have to establish procedures for getting that immunity in Washington, and it would be an interesting problem for the lawyers. So far we've been talking primarily about price disclosure. Are there other information dimensions?

MR. SIERS: I think it's important that all of us recognize, as Fred has said, that we've been focusing primarily on price disclosure. I think there is equal concern as regards cost disclosure. And I'm thinking primarily for example of our manufacturing costs and our types of process operations. The type of process can pretty well be determined by people who are knowledgeable concerning your manufacturing costs. Our advertising cost is another area where disclosure would, in my opinion, be essentially telegraphing your plans to your competitor. And, much more important, is the extent to which you are required to report research and development expense and the manner in which this is being spent. That's a clear message to your competitor on exactly what your plans are for the future. So disclosures of these types of information are of equal, if not of more, concern to me than price disclosures.

MR. MILLSTEIN: I've heard rumors to the effect that people spend hundreds of thousands of dollars to develop this sort of information about one another simply because it is so competitively interesting to know what your competitor's costs, labor rates, etc., are; and here we're talking about government programs that may lay all this out.

MR. ROWE: We've talked about this paradox of disclosure by the government having chilling effects on competition under traditional antitrust concepts. But can't we eliminate this antitrust competitive paradox, perhaps by providing for individual company disclosure to the government or to a neutral third party on a confidential basis, and with the disclosure to the public only on the basis of some information aggregate?

MR. MILLSTEIN: Well, now you're changing the ground rules because, and I think that everybody ought to know what we're doing, we're shifting away from the matter of the disclosure of individual company data — there, at least I understand the argument. I don't find I'm necessarily sympathetic with all of it, but I understand the "corporate constituency" argument that individual company disclosure may be a good thing. But the question I now see is: Can't we solve the individual company data confidentiality problem by putting the data in the bank, not allowing anybody ever to look at it, and disclosing only industry aggregates. For what purpose would you aggregate?

MR. DAM: Isn't the purpose obvious? It's really related to a particular economic theory: namely, a structuralist theory that posits a particular association, a particular correlation, between concentration and profits. That's what the aggregate data are useful in testing.

MR. MILLSTEIN: Is this structuralist theory accepted? My own statement of the structural theory would be that it is intended to substitute mechanical standards of competitiveness for the very arduous quest for behavior and performance that we've traditionally insisted upon in antitrust matters.

In other words, you draw conclusions about the state of competition in a market based on the number of companies in the market. I don't find any support for this in antitrust law or policy. I've always read the antitrust laws as preventing certain types of behavior such as restraint of trade and monopolization, but not concentration or bigness. It is shocking to think that a big antitrust case could be conclusively resolved just by finding that four companies have a given percent of a given market.

MR. DAM: I agree. There's a question about what the antitrust laws mean, but there's a broader question about what public policy for concentrated industries should be. Perhaps, for example, there might be a legislative change. I have the most serious doubts about these structuralist theories, particularly given some of the work that's been done in recent years by people such as Yale Brozen at my own university. His study, for example, has shown that whatever the relationship between concentration and profits may be, it doesn't persist over time. But, as a responsible academic, I could hardly say that we shouldn't try to test the theory. If it doesn't prove out, then it doesn't prove out, and we can dispose of it once and for all.

MR. MILLSTEIN: That is probably one of the most bothersome arguments about collecting this kind of data because when we encounter some responsible academic who doesn't believe in the structural theory, he says: "Well I don't believe in the structuralist theory, but I sure would like to get my hands on that data because I'd prove the structuralist theory was wrong." I think, however, the government mechanism is rolling into effect to prove a theory rather than to test it. I think the theory has spawned the need for the information.

MR. DAM: But you have to have a hypothesis before you can test it. Earlier we said one of the problems was collecting data where you didn't know what the question was. We now know what the question is: is there an association between concentration and profits, or isn't there? So you say let's go ahead and collect the data and let's see whether or not, as a responsible academic, you'll test whether there is such a thing as a structuralist theory.

MR. ROWE: Can you disprove the theory?

MR. MILLSTEIN: Well, supposing we had responsible economists from all persuasions get together and create a program and announce to the world that the reason for the program was really not to prove that four companies having fifty percent of an industry was automatically a bad thing, but to find whether any positive relationships existed — is there a relationship between concentration and profits, and if so is it due to collusion or efficiency? Is there a relationship between concentration and advertising, and if so is it due to a bias in the use of accounting data or to some competitively significant factor? Supposing they convinced us all that that's what they wanted to do.

I venture to say that if industry were convinced that a rational, non-prosecutorial, fair-minded group of experts set about to engage in bona fide research, not to prove the theory, but to examine the current issues, to examine all of the competing theories and then begin to see whether any meaningful relationships existed between concentration and advertising and inflation and profitability and the like, I think the opposition would begin to evaporate and I think that it might be replaced by a cooperative attitude.

And I think that all the contestants in this great war which has developed would begin to step back and take another look at it. Now the problem that we have is that we have a program instituted not to test anything. Instead, it's being started immediately to plan antitrust enforcement and to help win cases for the government. Those are the stated purposes of the programs which the FTC is undertaking. Indeed, the current acting chairman of the commission has called this the greatest step forward in the antitrust field that's occurred in his lifetime.

How can responsible academics look at what is going on and support these programs when the whole purpose is to use the information immediately — to put it into play, put it out for use, use it in cases — without regard to whether or not the information does or doesn't demonstrate the basis of the structural theory? Now, it seems to me responsible academics ought to be rising up and screaming about this instead of saying, well, let them go and collect the data and we'll all play with it. That's my problem.

MR. ROWE: Ira, let's assume that you abolish the Federal Trade Commission, and you shift the question to Chicago where sunshine prevails. There you convene ten wise men who are impartial, dispassionate and profound, to play with this information. Still, is there a quality level of the data that will permit those neutral wise men to come out with a rational judgment as to whether the structuralist theory is valid or invalid?

MR. SIERS: I think that's a good question and one that ought to be of real concern to all of us. Let me say first that the line-of-business concept that has been advanced by the Federal Trade Commission is rapidly maturing. We're seeing it proliferating. We're seeing it worked into renegotiation. We're seeing it worked into the International Investment Survey Act, which will empower the Department of Commerce to collect information worldwide. We don't know where it's going to stop and everybody is just referring to "line of business" without really understanding what line of business is.

And I think there's a serious question about the quality of the line-of-business data. A lot of us have researched the proposed lines of business. Generally speaking, they all take off from the Standard Industrial Classification categories, which are really the only things that people can find that even begin to approach a market definition. But in truth, the Standard Industrial Classification Code is not the answer. First, it's a very broad classification, and most importantly, it's a manufacturing-oriented code structure, not a market-oriented code structure. Let me give you some examples. FTC Code 35.37, miscellaneous non-electrical machinery, includes engine valves, internal combustion engine filters, weather vanes, and merry-go-rounds. FTC Code 37.14, miscellaneous transportation equipment, includes all terrain vehicles; automobile trailer chassis, except house trailers; golf-caddy carts; midget autos; and pushcarts.

Now how in the world does this define a market? So we have serious concern that no real work has ever been accomplished in defining markets and that's what this is all about. Before you start making any judgements on market participation, you have to define the markets, and right now we're just grabbing something that exists that is not appropriate to the purpose to which it's being put.

Secondly, even if the markets were right, then we have the noncomparability of the data. For example, I mentioned the various accounting conventions that companies are free to select. They don't select these in order to make a mess out of the line-of-business reporting. They select these accounting conventions based on their intelligent analysis and interpretation of what is best for their own individual companies. And then you have these individual information systems tailored to the organization and structure of the individual company. So you put all of this together and then aggregate noncomparable data to nonexistent markets and that's line of business.

MR. ROWE: Howard, you talked about these four-digit census categories, with their separation between the sweet-pickle category and sour-pickle category. What if you moved away from the four-digits to the three-digits, or maybe the two-digits, would the points which you have made still apply?

MR. SIERS: I think it's dangerous to generalize, and this is a point that I undoubtedly should have made at the start. Some companies, depending on their structure or on their product makeup, can fit comfortably in the four-digit structure. Other companies can fit comfortably in the two-digit structure. But again, you're always working away from a manufacturing-oriented structure. What we really need is some honest research on market definition. It's my understanding, certainly in an antitrust situation, that the first and most difficult thing to accomplish is to define the market, and yet we're just grabbing and saying, that's a market.

I don't know that two-digit is any better than four-digit. Two-digit for example would be food and kindred products. That's quite a wide range, so I don't think that's the answer. I think it takes more research.

MR. MILLSTEIN: I think the problem is that the people who jumped into line of business wanted to accomplish a miracle overnight. I don't think that what Howard, nor anybody responsible in the business community, is saying is that, categorically, it can't ever be done. I think the problem is that the information does not jump up at you ready-made — it isn't there. The tools aren't there yet to work with and what I think is misunderstood is the business community's objections to proceeding with the makeshift things that are lying around which will be used in the program.

The main objection is to the notion of playing around with half thought through ideas. Why? Because you are dealing with such a serious business. This isn't a question of using data to develop a trend like the GNP, or something of the sort. We're not talking about global figures for global policy planning. From this, you may die. On the basis of this information and the unproven structuralist theory it's to be used in conjunction with, you may be divested, dissolved — or whatever happens to you as a result of being in a concentrated industry which may have high accounting profits, or whatever.

MR. DAM: But you may be divested whether we have any information or not.

MR. MILLSTEIN: That's true, but why make it easy by using silly market codes? It seems to me that we ought to begin with defining the markets. Have you ever heard of an antitrust problem that doesn't begin with defining the market? Here, the most important antitrust program in history, according to some, is being conducted without defining markets. I don't know why people say the concerns about line of business are complicated.

If I stopped right there that should be enough. How can you have a big antitrust policy-planning program if you won't define a market? What's the point of publishing information for a code that is made up of engine valves and merry-go-rounds? It is absurd, I don't understand it.

MR. DAM: I'm glad to see that you don't think it's impossible in principle because, I venture to say, there never has been a statistical series of any kind that had no bugs in it, and yet we use statistical data all the time for public-policy decisions.

MR. ROWE: Are you saying, Ira, that this would be giving bad information to bad people for bad purposes? Ken is saying there's a possibility that somewhere out there, maybe in the suburbs of Chicago, there might exist an impartial body of dispassionate people who might possibly mush around and come out with something that would be not totally negative.

MR. MILLSTEIN: Well, knowing economists, I've learned that nothing is impossible. But when I think of the care that the government and a defendant will expend trying to establish what a particular market is in a particular antitrust case, and I compare that to taking a three- or four-digit SIC code and saying, that's a market and we're going to collect information for that so-called market and dump it, grind it into a computer, push a button and decide whether that so-called market is a proper antitrust target, it doesn't make any sense.

Now, another argument is that when all the numbers are in, it will all be published. When it's all published, your group will decide what the biases are, and you'll go to work on it and explain it's no good, and my group will explain how wonderful it is and we'll have a war. So really, nothing bad is going to come from the information because we'll fight about its value later on.

MR. ROWE: And the truth shall make you free.

MR. MILLSTEIN: And the truth shall make us free, right. My problem with that is a little allegory I would like to tell about the $80 billion number that was in the newspapers as the cost of price fixing. I'd like to tell you how it all came about.

Once upon a time, there was an economist who in a chapter of a textbook he wrote took a guess at what he estimated to be the social losses from ineffective competition as of 1966. He hedged that estimate with very carefully expressed caveats; he really did. He noted that his calculation was "inherently 'iffy' and subjective," and that it had to be taken with "the appropriate grain of salt."[6] And he later stated that in developing this $80 billion number, he "threw all scholarly caution to the wind."[7]

Following that number in a chapter of a book, along came an Antitrust Division chief to state that "the price tag for inefficient competition in America resulting from market structures and illegal anticompetitive conduct could run as high as $80 billion"[8]; and that received some publicity. Much more than the book had. Still later, in the *Congressional Record,* it became "price fixing and other anticompetitive actions [that] raise price levels by as much as $80 billion a year."[9] Still later, in a publication, it became inefficiency resulting from corporate monopoly that cost $80 billion.[10] Most recently, the ante was up, probably because of inflation, to $87 billion as representing the Federal Trade Commission's price tag on oligopoly.[11]

My conclusion is, you have no more hope of ever catching up with the published results in the line-of-business program than you do of catching up with the $80 billion number. The numbers, as bad as they may be, will never come to rest. And that's the problem with bad numbers. You don't ever catch up with them.

As big as business is, it doesn't have the access to the press that a Congressman, a Senator, a head of the Antitrust Division, a Chairman of the Federal Trade Commission has, when they begin to rattle out data. And it seems to me it explains in words of one syllable why the business community is afraid of bad numbers — they will never catch up with them. They'll run away; they'll be used against companies; they will show up in cases; they'll show up in Congressional findings; they'll show up in preambles to legislation; they'll show up everywhere. You never catch up with them. I really think this is the essential problem calling for legitimate concern about this kind of an approach.

MR. ROWE: Ira, you've spoken about the fact that the truth really will not make you free, because you will never be in a position to catch up with the untruth. Apart from that aspect of it, is there another side effect that bad information might be utilized to achieve purposes contrary to the purposes professed to be achieved by the data collection in the first place?

MR. MILLSTEIN: Really one of the more serious problems is that people like Ken will never have access to the data, and that bothers me. Ken, you had some thoughts about that.

MR. DAM: The point is that independent economists and lawyers won't be able to go behind the data summaries by, in this case, the Federal Trade Commission to find out how the raw data were collected and, therefore, won't be able to test fully the validity of conclusions that might rest on faulty data.

MR. MILLSTEIN: One of the problems is the differences among companies, as Howard has explained. How will we ever find out what those differences are and how they may have contributed to biases and errors? These are the problems that show up, and that is why I think it is so incumbent on industry not only to be concerned but to think about how to solve the problems.

I think we should put the beginning of the discussion together with the end. If the development of information seems inevitable and the current programs don't solve the problems, it won't be left as a stalemate. Life isn't like that.

MR. ROWE: I think you're quite right, Ira. The time has come to try to put some of the beginnings and the ends together.

Today's discussion has pointed out some of the dilemmas which are posed by the disclosure of operating data by large corporations in an open democratic society which is traditionally information addicted, and now waxing giddy on electronic data processing. Clearly information has an economic and social cost and price, which must be seen and must be weighed in the policy balance in light of the particular aims to be achieved.

Haunting paradoxes do arise in the world of antitrust, where too much information may chill competitive moves. Also, confidentiality and aggregation are not panaceas. Aggregation may only expose more clearly the clash between structuralist preconceptions about industries and markets, and the fluid diversity of competitive business which defies static formulas and categorizations.

In the end, the medium may be the message. The structuralist answer may precede and predefine the information question, giving early warning signals for broader collisions between planning, regulation and competition.

Whatever else appeared from the discussion, it seems plain that we are now faced with a policy impasse on corporate disclosure, at the same time as we're being engulfed by a rising tide of information. To a large extent we may be victimized by those economists who profess certitude from numbers and constructs as the key to far-reaching policy decisions.

But whatever is asserted as the justification for compelling business information and disclosure, I think one should and must appropriately insist on rationality, meaningful cost-benefit demonstrations, backed by a persuasive statement of need in terms of relevance and of significance for a disclosed and for an acceptable policy decisional process.

Today the issues are polarized by litigation, adversary confrontations, and the clamor of an election year. Tomorrow's challenge may be whether the business community can take broad and positive initiatives on the information front, or pay the heavy price of losing the public opinion war.

[1] Biographies of the speakers are found on pp. 103-105.

[2] M. Green, R. Nader, and J. Seligman, *Constitutionalizing The Corporation: The Case for the Federal Chartering of Giant Corporations* (1976).

[3] *Ibid* at 215 to 293.

[4] See, for example, Patrick J. Davey and John I. Porter, *Inventory Accounting Policies: The Trend to LIFO,* Conference Board Information Bulletin No. 4, December 1975.

[5] See, for example, Stanley J. PoKempner and Rochelle O'Connor, editors, *Senior Management and the Data Processing Function,* Conference Board Report No. 636, 1974.

[6] F.M. Scherer, *Industrial Market Structure and Economic Performance* (Rand McNally & Co., 1970), p. 408. Dr. Scherer is now Director of the FTC's Bureau of Economics.

[7] "Monopoly the Villain: Trust-Busting Has Become a Weapon Against Inflation," *Barron's,* Nov. 4, 1974, at 9.

[8] BNA, *Antitrust & Trade Regulation Report,* A-7 (Aug. 8, 1974).

[9] 121 Cong. Rec. S 378 (daily ed. January 17, 1975); see also 121 Cong. Rec. S 10731 (daily ed. June 17, 1975), where Senator Hart stated: ". . . $80 billion. That is how much the lack of competition in our economy costs, as estimated by Assistant Attorney General for Antitrust, Thomas Kauper."

[10] R. Estes, "The $80 Billion Misunderstanding," *MONOGRAM* 31 (Jan.-Feb. 1976).

[11] *Ibid.*

ANTITRUST IN
THE UNITED STATES:

A View for Europeans

Consistency and Change in Antitrust in the United States: An Introduction

Betty Bock

WHILE THE BROAD purposes underlying the U.S. antitrust laws have remained the same since the Sherman Act was passed in 1890, the companies and industries that shape the economy have been undergoing continuing change. Thus, in 1890 our economy was made up in large part of small, single-product, local and regional firms menaced by combinations – or trusts – in such industries as oil, steel, tobacco and sugar. The Sherman Act was, therefore, directed at the problems of regional and local mangements that needed protection if they were not to be swept away or swept into the growing national trusts. Thus, the Sherman Act, prohibiting conspiracies and monopolization or intent to monopolize, was broadly framed, in order to leave to the courts the opportunity to formulate the specific meaning of the law in the light of Congress's broad faith in multiple independent companies as the underlying strength of a competitive enterprise system.

Thus, the Sherman Act, fortified by the Clayton Act and the Federal Trade Commission Act of 1914, by the Robinson-Patman Act and Wheeler-Lea Amendment to the Federal Trade Commission Act in 1936, and by the Merger Act of 1950 – as well as by other laws affecting specific sectors of the economy – has carried forward a national conviction that a minimum of government and private regulation and a maximum of competition would give our economy the best possible opportunity to meet the growing needs of a population that has continuously looked ahead to higher and more diversified standards of living.

But neither in 1890 nor in the later supplementary legislation was systematic analysis focused on the relations between the basic purposes of antitrust and what are today – over three-quarters of a century later – such grave national problems as inflation combined with high unemployment, shortage and excess capacity, and the growth of multinational enterprises. Nor could those who framed the antitrust laws take account of the changing competitive conditions and practices that would, decade after decade, shape different industries in varying ways. They could foresee change, but not the detailed direction of change and, therefore, left the specific guidance of the enterprise system to the independent judgment of private enterprise, the obligations of the antitrust enforcement agencies, and the wisdom of the judicial process.

It follows that the laws have not developed in monolithic form but, by now, impinge in varying patterns on virtually the entire range of corporate structure and practices – among them, for example – the number and shares of major competitors in a market; agreements among competitors; corporate decisions concerning growth by internal investment or by acquisition; corporate decisions to deal, or not to deal, with particular suppliers, distributors or outlets; pricing methods, discount schedules, and the terms of contracts with suppliers or customers; licensing terms; and the overarching implications of the operations of multinational corporations.

Charted and Uncharted Areas

In this setting, the decided antitrust cases can be likened to discontinuous contour lines on a topological map, where the lines are widely spaced and − in some places − lacking. This is so because there are specific corporate activities that *plainly* violate − or do not violate − the law. But there are ranges of activity that lie in unmapped regions where the form and substance of the action and the nature of the markets affected determine whether an antitrust problem exists.

This is so because it is part of the canon of antitrust that too much competition destroys competition; too little creates a passive industry that does not serve the public interest. And both too much and too little violate the law. Too much can be exemplified by a long-drawn-out program of sales below cost designed to drive out competitors and so to monopolize a market; too little can be exemplified by agreements not to sell in a competitor's trade area. Less clear is *what "too much" or "too little" competition means in a complex economy.*

For example, although monopolization violates Section 2 of the Sherman Act, one may ask under what conditions monopolization begins in the course of the growth of a strong innovative company − or what forms or methods of growth are compatible with competition − whatever the outcome. Or, conversely, although agreements in restraint of trade violate Section 2 of the Sherman Act, one may ask what types of simultaneous action by independent companies represent such agreements, as distinct from individual company responses to similar competitive opportunities and constraints.

Problems for antitrust practitioners are, therefore, marked not only by such antinomies, but by the fact that today, more fully than ever before in peacetime, we in the United States have a mixed economy in which the government imposes greater or lesser degrees of explicit and implicit regulation to which private industry must adjust, while planning for the future as independently as changing regulation will permit. The result is a series of *ad hoc* actions and reactions by government and private enterprise that tend to generate *unforeseeable long-range problems* in the course of attempts to solve *short-range problems that are all too visible.*

We have, for example, tried to strengthen our welfare and educational systems without reformulating long-range goals. We have established stringent rules concerning corporate responsibility for environmental and product safety, without long-range analysis of how the costs will affect levels of prices, demand and corporate ability to invest. We have mounted attacks on large-scale producers, without exploring whether, for some products, only mass production can underwrite low costs for successive generations of mass-consumed output. Nor have we given detailed consideration to the conditions under which forced reduction in the capacity of major companies − called restructuring in the bills that have been introduced in Congress − might raise unit costs of production and distort the distribution of what the U.S. enterprise system *could* produce.

40

Not surprisingly, our attitudes toward competition from abroad are marked by similar disjunctions between short- and long-range purposes. Thus, while the Antitrust Division of the Department of Justice takes a positive stand toward imports and foreign investment in the United States as a check on the prices of domestically produced output and as an incentive toward domestic innovation and efficiency, Congress, the Department of the Treasury, and the U.S. International Trade Commission are concerned when foreign imports or investment are perceived as creating domestic unemployment. Thus if a foreign company is selling in the United States at prices lower than those at which it is selling in other markets, surcharges on what it is exporting into the United States can be assessed.

The moral here is simple — and will be repeated in more concrete form in the papers that follow: we welcome competition — including foreign competition — that gives us new price and product alternatives, and induces new efficiencies, but we are committed to fostering domestic industries, domestic employment, and the domestic economy.

Structuralism vs. Realism

This basic paradox is paralleled by a second set of paradoxes generated by a revival of 19th century populism side by side with an emerging 20th century realism. Thus, today, a part of Congress and of the economics profession hold that bigness is bad; smallness, good. This mode of thought — developed in an era when the United States had wide frontiers, a small population, and no mass production — equated bigness with "power" and smallness with a lack of "power." And possession of power, without more, was wrong. This view, in its modern form, can be called a "structuralist" one. A differing and emerging way of looking at today's competitive problems can be characterized as a "realist" view.

Under the structuralist view, large corporate size automatically spells undue power — and high concentration (when a few companies account for a high share of market sales) also automatically spells undue power — for which structuralists find few, if any, economic or legal justifications.

Under the realist view, competitive facts — not size or market share numbers — are the test of whether or not given corporate activities are competitive. The realists, therefore, argue that there should normally be room for consideration of facts concerning whether a given corporate practice or market structure is pro-competitive, anticompetitive or neutral.

The strength of the structuralist approach lies in its appeal to elementary fears of what we do not understand; and in its support in some segments of Congress, the antitrust enforcement agencies, and the United States Supreme Court's antitrust decisions of the 1960's. The strength of the realist approach lies in the growing support of the Supreme Court of the 1970's and of scholars who have questioned the validity of market share and concentration figures, standing alone. Indeed, in such decisions as *General Dynamics,*[1] *Marine Bancorporation,*[2] and *Citizens and Southern,*[3] a majority of the Supreme Court has considered specific competitive circumstances and has refused to base its conclusions on bare numerical abstractions.

If we in the United States come to value *generalized answers to political-economic questions* more highly than specific ones, the gap between the structuralists and the realists will widen. But if we come to value *precision in analysis of the technical-economic problems* that lie at the core of our production and delivery systems in different markets, the gap will narrow. How the interplay will affect European companies doing business in the United States — and American companies as well — will depend on their own actions, the markets in which they operate, and how the debate works itself out with respect to individual issues.

Opportunities and Risks for Non-U.S. Management

For the foreign company doing business in the United States, the importance of understanding such issues is greater, the greater the company's absolute size in worldwide terms and the greater its potential impact on competition in the United States. The non-U.S. company's standing under the U.S. antitrust laws becomes better in proportion as its activities promote real and needed competition, particularly in scarce resources or in products or services that are in short supply. And such a company's standing before the Department of Justice increases when the company seeks to enter a concentrated U.S. market, provided it enters through its own expansion; or through an acquisition of one of the smaller or less viable, rather than one of the larger or stronger, companies in the markets it is entering.

Conversely, a foreign company's standing under the U.S. antitrust laws decreases in proportion as its activities provide excessive competition or if it enters agreements to lessen competition between itself and other companies selling into, or operating in, the United States. Its problems are particularly great if it is enticed by its own volume-cost relationships, by exchange rates — or both — to sell in the United States at prices below those at which it sells comparable products elsewhere and, in the process, creates U.S. unemployment traceable to such pricing.

To repeat — the touchstone here is the fact that in principle, we in the United States welcome competition, but we also discourage competition that reduces opportunities for competition in the future. The practical significance of this attitude is that, regardless of its consistency or inconsistency, it comes close to providing an equal-opportunity rule for U.S. and non-U.S. competitors in the United States.

The papers that follow explore various manifestations of this rule. A. Paul Victor of the New York City law firm of Weil, Gotshal & Manges, considers mergers, acquisitions and joint ventures involving a foreign firm; Paul H. LaRue, of Chadwell, Kayser, Ruggles, McGee & Hastings in Chicago, Illinois, considers exporting and selling in the United States — pricing and distribution; and James H. Wallace, Jr., of Kirkland, Ellis & Rowe in Washington, D.C., considers the United States as a land of licensing opportunity.

James A. Rahl, Dean of the Northwestern University School of Law in Chicago, Illinois, and Allen C. Holmes, of Jones, Day, Reavis & Pogue in Cleveland, Ohio, present overviews of the direction of U.S. antitrust law, in terms of the problems of the multinational; and Miles W. Kirkpatrick, of Morgan, Lewis & Bockius in Washington, D.C., outlines new departures in trade regulation enforcement.

[1] *General Dynamics Corp., U.S. v.* (US S Ct 1974) 1974 *Trade Cases,* Par. 74,967.

[2] *Marine Bancorporation, Inc., U.S. v.* (US S Ct 1974) 1974 *Trade Cases,* Par. 75,125.

[3] *Citizens and Southern National Bank, U.S. v.* (US S Ct 1975) 1975 *Trade Cases,* Par. 60,360.

Mergers, Acquisitions and Joint Ventures Involving a Foreign Firm

A. Paul Victor*

THIS PAPER ATTEMPTS to provide a limited briefing concerning the U.S. antitrust implications of mergers, acquisitions and joint ventures involving a foreign firm. Since the subject is broad, a limited scanning of the most significant points is, however, all that can be attempted.

For present purposes, I think it can be presumed that *any agreement or combination,* regardless of its form, which results in the creation of a new company — or the absorption or control by one company of another — under any one of the following circumstances will be subject to scrutiny under the U.S. antitrust laws *if* an American company is involved, *or* the domestic or foreign commerce of the United States will be affected: if the companies are actual or potential competitors; if the companies are in a vertical relationship (such as customer and supplier); or if the companies are in unrelated fields but there is a reasonable probability of anticompetitive impact.

Since such transactions involve some form of agreement between two or more companies, their antitrust implications should be tested under Sections 1 and 2 of the Sherman Act,[1] Section 7 of the Clayton Act,[2] and Section 5 of the Federal Trade Commission Act.[3] A brief review of those statutes will show their differences in subject matter and jurisdiction.

Section 1 of the Sherman Act prohibits all combinations, conspiracies or contracts in restraint of trade or commerce among the several states, or with foreign nations. Section 2 condemns monopolization, attempts to monopolize, or combinations and conspiracies to monopolize *any part* of the *same* trade or commerce. Unlike Section 7 of the Clayton Act, the Sherman Act applies to *all* persons, whether corporations or not; applies to all activities *affecting* commerce; and requires an *actual* restraint of trade before a violation can be found.[4] Its potential reach over transactions involving foreign companies is broader than Section 7, but the need for an actual restraint of trade makes evidence for its application more demanding than when the alleged unlawful conduct *simply* involves a merger.

Section 7, by contrast, condemns anticompetitive acquisitions of the stock or assets by one "corporation engaged in commerce" of another "corporation also engaged in commerce." Since it applies *only* to corporate transactions, its juris-

*Partner, law firm of Weil, Gotshal & Manges, New York, N.Y.

45

dictional reach is more limited than the Sherman Act's, although the criteria for establishing a violation are less strict. However, the "commerce" in which such corporations must be engaged is "trade or commerce among the several states and with foreign nations." Whether Section 7 can apply to a *purely foreign merger, or to a merger in which the foreign company had nothing whatsoever to do with the United States market* is an open question. Two recent Supreme Court decisions, *Gulf Oil v. Copp*[5] and *United States v. American Building Maintenance*,[6] suggest that Section 7 would not apply. For example, although dealing with an acquisition between U.S. companies, the Court held in the *American Building* case that Section 7 does *not* encompass corporations engaged in intrastate activities which substantially affect interstate commerce. It covers only corporations engaged in the flow of interstate commerce. Nothing in the opinion suggests a different result if a foreign company is involved. There is, however, a move in Congress to overturn this restrictive interpretation of the scope of Section 7.

Because Section 7 also requires that the anticompetitive effects of an acquisition be demonstrated in a "section of the country," there is an open question as to whether an acquisition which involves solely the export trade of the United States could violate Section 7. Most antitrust students have concluded that such transactions will not ultimately enjoy Section 7 immunity.

By contrast to Section 7, Section 5 of the Federal Trade Commission (FTC) Act condemns "unfair methods of competition in commerce," with commerce again defined to include that "with foreign nations." The FTC has challenged mergers and acquisitions under Section 5, although usually in conjunction with a simultaneous attack under Section 7. Under Section 5, there is *no* requirement that the merging companies be *"engaged in"* commerce, as is required under Section 7. Nor is Section 5 applicable *only* to corporations. Moreover, Section 5 is a *super incipiency statute,* and can be invoked to prevent the mere threat of a lessening of competition or the elimination of potential competition. It is potentially the broadest statute under which a merger or acquisition can be challenged. Indeed, the FTC recently acted under Section 5 to challenge several purely foreign acquisitions in the ball bearing industry, as part of a complaint which also attacked related acquisitions and transactions involving U.S. companies. This was the *SKF Industries* complaint filed in July, 1975.[7]

But although private parties can challenge a merger under Section 7, they cannot invoke Section 5. Only the FTC can do so, and this may be an important moderating factor in enforcement, particularly when foreign ramifications are involved.

One other "jurisdictional" point should not be forgotten. If stock of a corporation is acquired *only* for investment purposes, Section 7 will not apply. That provision is in the statute itself. But beware — the term "investment" is not defined, and the cases make it clear that where a stockholder — even a small minority stockholder — is in a position to exercise control over the management of the acquired company, or where an intent to obtain such control is shown, or where such stock ownership influences the corporation's conduct in an anticompetitive manner, Section 7 will apply.

Let us now consider Section 7 as it applies to transactions involving a foreign company. Section 7 condemns corporate acquisitions where the effect may be substantially to lessen competition or to tend to create a monopoly in any line of commerce in any section of the country. Section 7 looks to the future in an effort to stop restraints of trade at an early stage, and mergers will be held unlawful if there is a reasonable probability that they will produce anti-competitive effects in a relevant market.

It should be made clear at the outset that the substantive criteria applicable under Section 7 to purely domestic mergers are similarly applicable where a foreign company is involved. There can be differences under certain circumstances, as Assistant Attorney General Thomas A. Kauper noted, for example, in testimony regarding the effect of currency devaluations or tariff changes on foreign companies seeking to acquire an American company. *Basically, however, we can confidently consult the criteria developed in domestic cases to assess the legal risks of a merger involving a foreign company.*

The first problem in *any* Section 7 case is product and geographic market definition because competitive effects can only be judged within a market framework. What are the relevant products and where are the relevant products sold by the acquired firm? Obviously, the chances of legality change as we look at different possible "markets" in which to measure the market "shares" of the merging parties; the higher the market share the more likely it is that illegality will be found.

As far as the "line of commerce" or product market is concerned, the Supreme Court has made it clear that a particular product may be part of more than one market. In other words, a broad market may contain submarkets in which the competitive effects of a merger must be evaluated.

In the landmark *Brown Shoe* case,[8] the Court held that the outer boundaries of a product market are drawn to include substitutes which are reasonably interchangeable in use or for which there is cross-elasticity of demand. Thus, although cellophane and glassine film are different products, they may be in a broad market for flexible packaging materials. But this broad market may also include several submarkets, depending on such factors as industry or public recognition of the submarket as a separate economic entity, the products' peculiar characteristics and uses, unique production facilities, distinct prices, and the like. And illegality will follow if the adverse competitive effects are discernable in any one market.[9]

As for geographic markets — that is the "section of the country" in which the merger will be appraised — an area of effective competition must be established. It can be nationwide,[10] statewide[11] or citywide,[12] or a combination thereof — all such geographic markets have already been upheld by the Supreme Court. Again, a violation in only *one* market is enough to create liability.

Now, let's examine the anticompetitive effects required to find a violation in the case of horizontal, vertical or conglomerate mergers.

Until recently, courts would probably condemn horizontal mergers involving firms which are actual competitors on the basis of market share and concentration statistics alone. In other words, structural data, rather than a realistic analysis of competition, were all-important. This approach is also reflected in the Justice Department's *Merger Guidelines* where, for example, it is indicated that in a market where the shares of the four largest firms equal less than 75 percent, the Department will ordinarily challenge a horizontal acquisition between firms each of whose market shares approximate 5 percent.[13]

But the days of a simple structural analysis may well be coming to an end. In 1974, a five-member majority of the Supreme Court took a much more tolerant view of a horizontal merger in the *General Dynamics* case.[14] The case concerned two coal companies that had combined sales amounting to more than 20 percent of the relevant market, a share that would probably be held illegal if amassed by acquisition. But because the acquired company was short of the coal reserves required to compete in the future — that is, short of competitive potential — the Court allowed the merger, stressing factors other than market shares, rank in industry, concentration or other structural data concerning the merging companies. In other words, the realities of competition in the marketplace were considered.

Again in 1975, in the *Citizens and Southern National Bank* case,[15] the government's demonstration of high market shares by an acquiring bank simply shifted the burden to the defendant to prove that such market share statistics "gave an inaccurate account of the acquisitions' probable effects on competition," citing *General Dynamics*. It looks like a new ball game in the field of horizontal mergers, where the numbers game alone will no longer reign supreme.

As for vertical mergers, the principal evil is the possible foreclosure of competitors of either party from a part of the market previously open to them.[16] The *Brown Shoe* case concerned Section 7 condemnation of the acquisition by Brown, a shoe manufacturer, of Kinney, a shoe retailer.[17] The share of the retail shoe market foreclosed to competing shoe manufacturers by the acquisition was only about two percent, but Kinney had been the largest independent shoe chain in the country. Furthermore, there had been a definite trend toward vertical integration in the shoe industry, with the result that the available outlets were "drying up" for independent shoe producers. Finally, Brown itself had been a moving factor in this trend, having made several other acquisitions. Hence, illegality was found.

Although later decisions have shown the same tendency to condemn vertical mergers as *Brown Shoe,* it is not clear how much the Supreme Court's *General Dynamics* thinking will also influence *vertical* merger analysis. However, one can speculate that the Court is likely in the future to consider more than just market shares in vertical cases as well.

In the face of restrictive rules governing horizontal and vertical mergers, it is hardly surprising that merger-minded companies turned their attention to so-called conglomerate transactions, where the merging companies are neither competitors, nor suppliers, nor customers. This subject is of paramount interest to foreign companies seeking to diversify geographically into the United States, since "market extension" mergers are characterized as "conglomerate" transactions.

Probably the most discussed conglomerate concept concerns "potential competition." Since Section 7 looks to the future, a merger which eliminates a potential competitor may under certain circumstances violate the statute.

In its simplest form, potential competition focuses on the loss of the acquiring company as a probable entrant into the relevant market by internal expansion. A potential competitor, in this sense, is a company that would have come into the market by internal integration *but for* the acquisition. Important factors to consider in this regard are: internal memoranda or reports evidencing an intention to enter alone, the financial and technological capability to enter; the economic incentive to do so; and whether the market itself has room for a new entrant.

Once it is established that two merging companies *are* potential competitors, it is possible to predict the kind of adverse competitive impact that can lead to a finding of illegality. If the probable entrant would have been able to secure a *significant* share had it entered by means other than acquisition, then such competition has been eliminated by the merger. And if the market is a concentrated one, with relatively few sellers, the elimination of a substantial factor might, under traditional principles, lead to illegality.

Under another theory, expressed by the Supreme Court in the recent *Falstaff* case, if the firms in a highly concentrated market think that there is a strong firm waiting on the edge of the market for the appropriate time to enter, the existing companies will refrain from raising their prices to a level high enough to make it worthwhile for the potential entrant to risk coming in.[18] In other words, the threat of entry keeps prices down, and acquisitions which eliminate this threat can run afoul of Section 7.[19]

Under either the "but for" or the "perceived threat of entry" theories, the Supreme Court's decision last year in *Marine Bancorporation*[20] has broken the stride of this previously steadily expanding doctrine. Although that case is arguably distinguishable because it involved banks, it nevertheless should be carefully considered when potential competition questions arise.

For example, legal barriers to entry will now be viewed largely the same as economic entry barriers. In the bank case, state banking laws provided serious constraints on potential entry into various state markets, and this factor weighed heavily in the Court's analysis.

Further, the case suggests that the potential competition doctrine will be restricted to concentrated markets, and the influence of potential competition must be proven by performance as well as by structural data. It may well no longer be possible to premise a violation simply on what is "perceived" by existing competitors in the market. If there are no other feasible means to enter a market — and, indeed, even if there are, if such means will neither deconcentrate the market nor produce other significant procompetitive results — Section 7 may not be available to forestall mergers involving potential competition.

As for joint ventures, the Supreme Court held in the *Penn-Olin* case that Section 7 applies to joint ventures.[21] Further, Section 1 of the Sherman Act is frequently involved in joint venture complaints. Joint ventures will not be viewed under a *per se* illegality test, since more than market shares will be looked at. Joint venture transactions most frequently involve potential competition problems. The basic task in determining possible antitrust problems is to satisfy yourself that neither company would have, or could have, gone into the business alone. In seeking to establish this, let me remind you that the Supreme Court has rejected subjective intent as determinative, opting for more objective criteria, such as the financial strength and competitive ability of the companies involved, the economic incentive for entering the market alone, and the necessity for having participation by foreign interests.[22]

Insofar as joint ventures between American and foreign companies are concerned, encouragement is found in the comments of Assistant Attorney General Kauper in May 1974, when he noted that it has been made crystal clear that if " 'the size and risks of the project are so great that one company alone cannot undertake the project,' a joint venture will be held to be legal under the U.S. antitrust laws." He further stated that it is only "when the joint venture is proved to have been a device for suppressing individual competition which otherwise could or would have occurred or for excluding competitors that the transaction will raise serious problems under our antitrust laws." He pointed out that neither the Antitrust Division nor the Federal Trade Commission had prosecuted a single joint venture or bidding arrangement to sell to foreigners in at least 20 years, and that literally hundreds of *foreign* joint ventures were formed and operated successfully by Americans during that period.

What this means is that, as a practical matter, joint ventures between U.S. and foreign companies have a pretty good chance of surviving under the U.S. antitrust laws. But it is not all roses, since the U.S. Government has not shied away from attacking joint ventures with foreigners where deemed warranted, such as the Monsanto-Bayer joint venture (Mobay) for the production of isocyonates used in making urethane foam, where Monsanto consented to sell its interest in the joint venture to Bayer, and the more recent government challenges to the joint ventures involving the manufacture of plastics between Hercules and Mitsui Petrochemical, which was dissolved by consent, and between Brunswick and Yamaha in the outboard motor industry.

What if a foreign company is interested in making a tender offer for the stock of an American company, or otherwise seeks to get control? What special concerns must be considered from the standpoint of U.S. antitrust law, if the target company management decides to resist?

In this regard, a well-established weapon in the target company's arsenal is to use Section 7 as a basis for obtaining preliminary injunctive relief in a lawsuit which also typically includes other alleged improprieties, such as Securities Act violations. Not only the target company can institute such an action, but others who are interested may also have standing, such as did the licenser who sued to prevent its competitor from purchasing its license in the *Royal Crown Cola* case.[23]

As a practical matter, the preliminary injunction litigation itself will most likely dispose of the entire matter, despite the absence of a full adjudication of the merits. If the target company is able to obtain a preliminary injunction against further purchases of its stock, the takeover probably will be abandoned. On the other hand, if the injunction is denied, the so-called "raider" company will probably obtain some representation on the board of directors, gain some influence over the company's operations and business, and gain access to some confidential information. Once that happens, existing management's ability to retain complete control over the target company's affairs and operations naturally diminishes.

There is no magic to the antitrust issues involved in tender offer cases. They are quite similar to those we have discussed earlier, depending on the nature and business of the companies involved. It does not matter whether only U.S. companies are litigating or whether a foreign company is somehow involved, as the *Imetal-Copperweld*[24] and *Texasgulf Canada Development*[25] fights clearly attest.

What *does* matter is that the litigation will be decided under antitrust principles on the basis of standards other than the full merits of the legality of an acquisition under Section 7. The prevalent standard governing the issuance of preliminary injunctions balances the hardships to the parties and leans toward granting the injunction if the hardships tip decidedly in the plaintiff's favor and he has raised serious questions going to the merits which are "fair ground for litigation" and "deserve more deliberate investigation."[26] While some courts still do require plaintiffs to show a *reasonable probability* of a violation of Section 7,[27] the more recent trend appears to favor the plaintiff's position, with the burden of proving probable success somewhat reduced.

The target company has traditionally pointed to disruption of its personnel and customer and supplier relationships, the impairment of long-range planning and hiring capabilities, the likelihood of confidential data coming into the hands of a competitor, purchaser or supplier, and the risk of subsequent antitrust liabilities, in making its bid for court assistance. These factors, if reasonably apparent, seem to weigh more heavily than the probable loss of favorable market conditions that the acquiring company will ordinarily claim to establish its "irreparable injury."

This is not to suggest that the target company automatically prevails. Courts are cognizant that the antitrust claims must be real, not imagined. In the *Missouri Portland Cement-Cargill* case, the Court of Appeals noted that the Clayton Act was not enacted to provide a mechanism whereby entrenched management could block trading in its securities, unless the antitrust violation "was fairly clear" or the potential damage to the target company "decisively outweighed" that to the acquirer.[28] And in the *Texasgulf* case, which involved a foreign purchaser, the court rejected an antitrust-based effort to defeat the tender offer based on the Canadian buyer's alleged position as a likely potential entrant. It just wasn't so. So too, did the antitrust defense fail in the *Imetal* case.

In addition to defending on the merits, the acquiring company should not forget the possibility of urging some relief short of an injunction that will permit it to purchase a company's stock, although perhaps not exercise rights thereunder. In the *Vanadium* case, a limited order was entered by the court simply preventing the acquiring company's exercise of control even though the court noted strong evidence of a violation of Section 7.[29] Similarly, in the *MGM-Transamerica* litigation, the court designed an order which it felt would avoid the alleged possibility of control of the "raided" company by a major competitor, without preventing consummation of the acquisition.[30]

But other courts have been unconvinced of the viability of relief short of enjoining a tender offer. In *Gulf & Western*, the acquisition of A&P's stock was enjoined, although there was really no possibility that the target company would ever cooperate with the G&W interests.[31] And in the *Royal Crown Cola* case, the court refused "hold separate" relief as not being a practicable mechanism for preventing harm to the plaintiff or competition during the trial period.[32]

All in all, tender offer litigation is highly unpredictable. Nevertheless, the company attempting a takeover by tender offer must be sure to weigh the possibility of an antitrust-based defense. Conversely, where a company is defending against a tender offer, the antitrust laws may provide a truly effective mechanism for blocking the takeover and possibly defeating it once and for all without ever litigating fully on the merits.

As for the question of enforcement where there has been a merger involving a foreign party, I might point out that, until recent years, all such combinations had been attacked principally by the government, and only incidentally in lawsuits which were brought essentially to correct other unlawful Sherman Act activities, such as price fixing, market division, and the like. Such cases as *National Lead*[33] and *Timken Roller Bearing*[34] are representative of this category of cases. In recent years, however, mergers involving a foreign company have been challenged as themselves violating U.S. antitrust law, although not too many cases have actually been instituted. Still, enough have been litigated or settled to stand as a clear warning that careful review of proposed transactions is required, lest business plans be challenged. I need only refer to such cases as *Schlitz-Labatt*,[35] *British Petroleum-Sohio*,[36] *Litton-Triumph Adler*,[37] *CIBA-Geigy*[38] and *Nestle-Stauffer*[39].

There is also the possibility of *private* Section 7 actions for treble damages and injunctions. As you know, private antitrust actions have burgeoned in general, and there are recent indications that private Section 7 cases will likewise increase.

In private actions, the plaintiff has an additional problem that the government does not have — to demonstrate impact and injury to its business or property by reason of an unlawful acquisition before any relief can be granted. Moreover, the law is still developing as to what relief can be obtained by private parties — especially with respect to the propriety of divestiture prompted by private actions. Two cases on this point are the Ninth Circuit's *ITT-GTE*[40] decision and the Third Circuit's opinion in *Treadway-Brunswick*.[41] These Courts appear to have different views on the question of divestiture.

To sum up: when an acquisition involving foreign companies is contemplated, the implications under Section 7 of the Clayton Act, as well as under other antitrust provisions, should be examined. A foreign company will not ordinarily be treated any differently under the U.S. antitrust laws than its domestic counterpart. It should also be remembered that Section 7 of the Clayton Act is a two-way street. Just as "domestic merger" criteria apply to establish violations, such "domestic merger" defenses as the "failing company" and "toehold" defenses can apply to save a transaction where a foreign company is involved.

Despite their essentially market-structure approach, all potential transactions should initially be reviewed under the Justice Department's *Merger Guidelines*. But a more searching analysis, based on all relevant facts, should always be undertaken. Moreover, the recent Supreme Court decisions in *General Dynamics, Citizens and Southern National Bank,* and *Marine Bancorporation* may well mean that the realities of competition in an industry will be examined more closely from now on than the *Guidelines* themselves suggest. Also, if a proposed transaction involves sales or assets of $10 million or more and the combined companies have sales or assets exceeding $250 million, the FTC Merger Notification Requirements may well apply.

[1] 15 U.S.C. §§1, 2 (1970).

[2] 15 U.S.C. §18 (1970).

[3] 15 U.S.C. §45 (1970).

[4] *United States v. First Nat'l Bank & Trust Co.,* 376 U.S. 665 (1964).

[5] *Gulf Oil Corp. v. Copp Paving Co.,* 419 U.S. 186 (1974).

[6] *United States v. American Bldg. Maintenance Indus.,* 422 U.S. 271 (1975).

[7] *SKF Industries, Inc.,* Dkt. No. 9046 (F.T.C. July 22, 1975).

[8] *Brown Shoe Co. v. United States,* 370 U.S. 294 (1962).

[9] *United States v. E.I. du Pont de Nemours & Co.,* 351 U.S. 377 (1956).

[10] *Brown Shoe, supra.*

[11] *United States v. Pabst Brewing Co.,* 384 U.S. 546 (1966).

[12] *United States v. Von's Grocery Co.,* 384 U.S. 270 (1966).

[13] 1 C.C.H. Trade Reg. Rep. ¶4510 (1968).

[14] *United States v. General Dynamics Corp.,* 415 U.S. 486 (1974).

[15] *United States v. Citizens & S. Nat'l Bank,* 422 U.S. 86 (1975).

[16] See *Ford Motor Co. v. United States,* 405 U.S. 562 (1972).

[17] See note 8, *supra.*

[18] *United States v. Falstaff Brewing Corp.,* 410 U.S. 526 (1973).

[19] See *British Oxygen Co.,* 3 C.C.H. Trade Reg. Rep. ¶20,746 (F.T.C. 1974) (Initial decision).

[20] *United States v. Marine Bancorporation, Inc.,* 418 U.S. 602 (1974).

[21] *United States v. Penn-Olin Chem. Co.,* 378 U.S. 158 (1964).

[22] *Id.* at 167-8.

[23] *Royal Crown Cola v. Coca-Cola Bottling Midwest, Inc.,* 1972 Trade Cas. ¶74,266 (E.D. Wash. 1972).

[24] *Copperweld Corp. v. Imetal,* 1975-2 Trade Cas. ¶60,584 (W.D. Pa. Oct. 23, 1975).

[25] *Texasgulf, Inc. v. Canada Dev. Corp.,* 366 F. Supp. 374 (S.D. Tex. 1973).

[26] *Hamilton Watch Co. v. Benrus Watch Co.,* 206 F. 2d 738, 740 (2d Cir. 1953).

[27] *Briggs Mfg. Co. v. Crane Co.*, 185 F. Supp. 117 (E.D. Mich. 1960).

[28] *Missouri Portland Cement Co. v. Cargill, Inc.*, 489 F.2d 581 (2d Cir. 1974).

[29] *Vanadium Corp. of America v. Susquehanna Corp.*, 203 F. Supp. 686 (D. Del. 1962).

[30] *Metro-Goldwyn-Mayer, Inc. v. Transamerica Corp.*, 303 F. Supp. 1344 (S.D.N.Y. 1969).

[31] *Gulf & W. Indus. Inc. v. Great Atl. & Pac. Tea Co.*, 476 F.2d 687 (2d Cir. 1973).

[32] See note 23, *supra.*

[33] *United States v. National Lead Co.*, 332 U.S. 319 (1947).

[34] *Timken Roller Bearing Co. v. United States*, 341 U.S. 593 (1951).

[35] *United States v. Jos. Schlitz Brewing Co.*, 253 F. Supp. 129 (N.D. Cal.), *aff'd mem.*, 358 U.S. 37 (1966).

[36] *United States v. Standard Oil Co.*, 1970 Trade Cas. ¶72,988 (N.D. Ohio 1970).

[37] *Litton Indus., Inc.*, 3 C.C.H. Trade Reg. Rep. ¶ 20,267 (F.T.C. 1973) (Final order).

[38] *United States v. Ciba Corp.*, 1970 Trade Cas. ¶73,319 (S.D.N.Y. 1970).

[39] *Nestle Alimentana S.A.*, 3 C.C.H. Trade Reg. Rep. ¶20,808 (F.T.C. Jan. 7, 1975) (Complaint).

[40] *International Tel. & Tel. Corp. v. General Tel. & Electronics Corp.*, 518 F.2d 913 (9th Cir. Apr. 25, 1975).

[41] *NBO Indus. Treadway Cos. v. Brunswick Corp.*, 523 F.2d 262 (3d Cir. 1975), *cert. granted*, 22376 Feb. 23, 1976.

Exporting and Selling in the United States — Pricing and Distribution

Paul H. LaRue*

THE ROAD to compliance with the United States antitrust laws begins with an awareness and understanding of the ground rules applicable to pricing and distribution, as these are the areas of greatest antitrust activity and risk.

The policies underlying the pricing and distribution ground rules furnish a hint as to their general thrust. In the pricing area, the basic antitrust policy is to prevent any joint interference with the free play of market forces in the determination of prices.[1] Antitrust policy in the distribution area seeks to preserve the freedom of purchasers to buy in an open market.[2] All joint actions affecting prices and all restrictions upon product distribution are, therefore, suspect under United States antitrust law.

Now let us consider the pricing ground rules.

What the Exporter Should Be Concerned about in Pricing in the United States

Combinations of Competitors to Fix Prices

The exporter's principal concern in pricing should be to avoid any form of collusion with competitors. Price fixing among competitors is the cardinal sin of United States antitrust offenses, and it is dealt with harshly under the antitrust laws.

Price fixing has long been held to be illegal *per se* under Section 1 of the Sherman Act and Section 5 of the Federal Trade Commission Act. That is, it is conclusively presumed to be an unreasonable restraint of trade under the former statute and an unfair method of competition under the latter. Once a price-fixing combination has been found, no defense that its purpose was to eliminate competitive abuses or that the prices fixed were reasonable is permitted.[3]

The ban on price fixing is all-encompassing. As stated by the Supreme Court in *United States v. Socony-Vacuum Oil Co.*:

> "Under the Sherman Act a combination formed for the purpose and with the effect of raising, depressing, fixing, pegging, or stabilizing the price of a commodity in interstate or foreign commerce is illegal *per se.*"[4]

Combinations in which prices are fixed indirectly are prohibited as well as those in which they are fixed directly. In *Socony-Vacuum,* for example, the

*Partner, law firm of Chadwell, Kayser, Ruggles, McGee & Hastings, Chicago, Illinois.

illegal combination consisted of a joint program of the defendant refiners to purchase "distress" gasoline in order that the market price of regular gasoline would rise. Even a bare exchange of price information by competitors, without any agreement to adhere to specific prices, can amount to illegal price fixing if it stabilizes prices.

Since an express agreement need not be found in order to establish a price-fixing combination, such a combination being inferable from the conduct of the defendants and the surrounding circumstances, the exporter to the United States should refrain from all arrangements or discussions with competitors concerning prices.[5] It should neither exchange price lists with competitors, nor enter into any joint selling arrangement with them, such as through a common sales agency. There should be a firm, written policy, brought to the attention of all officers and sales personnel, that no one is to discuss prices with personnel of competitors either over the telephone, in correspondence, over the dinner table, or at trade association meetings.

Resale Price Maintenance

The exporter's second concern in the pricing area should be to refrain from any conduct in relation to its distributors or dealers in the United States that could be construed as resale price fixing. Although until recently sellers of trademarked commodities could lawfully stipulate and enforce resale prices in most states, the state fair trade laws legalizing this practice are fast on the way out. As part of the war on inflation, many of the state laws were repealed — fifteen during 1975 alone. As of November, 1975, only twenty-one states still had fair trade laws.[6] And legislation to repeal the two federal enabling statutes, signed by the President in December, 1975, will become effective March 11, 1976.

Without the antitrust immunity conferred by the fair trade laws, there is very little the exporter can lawfully do about its customers' resale prices. For the fixing of resale prices, bereft of this immunity, constitutes a *per se* violation of the Sherman[7] and Federal Trade Commission[8] Acts. This is so whether minimum or maximum resale prices are fixed, and irrespective of the form the resale price fixing takes.[9] For example, a refiner's practice of consigning gasoline to a large number of dealers, in order to control the retail price, has been condemned as illegal resale price fixing.[10] So has a seller's conditioning of discounts to wholesalers on their willingness to grant additional discounts to retailers.[11] And so, too, has General Foods' practice of contracting directly with institutional food accounts (such as hotel chains) and agreeing with them as to the prices at which they could purchase General Foods' products from distributors.[12] The court rejected the defense that since the distributors were not parties to the contracts, resale price fixing was not involved.

The so-called *"Colgate* doctrine," announced by the Supreme Court over fifty years ago, holds that a manufacturer does not violate the antitrust laws when it simply refuses to deal further with those who do not observe its suggested resale prices.[13] But subsequent Supreme Court decisions have made it clear that any action to enforce suggested resale prices beyond a simple refusal to deal is likely to result in a violation. Threats to terminate a price-cutting dealer to obtain its acquiescence to suggested resale prices, or the reinstatement of a former dealer upon a promise to refrain from further price cutting, are enough to establish an unlawful resale price-fixing combination.[14] Since it is almost impossible to walk the *Colgate* doctrine tightrope without losing one's footing, I regard the doctrine as too impractical to be the basis for a company's pricing policy. The most an exporter should do in regard to customers' resale prices, I believe, is to issue suggested resale prices while refraining from any effort to enforce them.

Prices Which Discriminate between Areas or Customers

Finally, in the area of pricing, the exporter should be aware of the possible legal implications of selling at lower prices in the United States than in its home market, or of engaging in price discrimination within the United States by charging different prices in different areas or to competing customers.

In common with the international community, the EEC, and many other nations, the United States prohibits "dumping."[15] The more frequently invoked of the two United States antidumping laws provides for the imposition of special "dumping duties" whenever an imported article is sold in the United States at less than "fair value" (*i.e.,* less than its home market price or cost of production) and an American industry is likely to be injured. In recent years, the number of proceedings brought under this law has increased dramatically. European Economic Community officials, complaining that over 20 percent of traditional Common Market exports to the United States are threatened by pending antidumping investigations, have expressed their concern to the Ford Administration.[16] Clearly, the exporter must reckon with the antidumping laws in pricing its products for sale in the United States.

Price discrimination within the United States is covered by the Robinson-Patman Act.[17] That statute is the most controversial of the federal antitrust laws, the main criticism being that it is at odds with the Sherman Act's policy of fostering vigorous price competition. In recent years there has been growing disenchantment with the Robinson-Patman Act, even at the Federal Trade Commission, the agency responsible for its enforcement, with the result that enforcement has come almost to a standstill. Additionally, the Ford Administration has proposed legislation to repeal or modify the Act substantially. Predictably, this proposed legislation drew immediate opposition from small business organizations and supporters of small business in Congress.

Regardless of current legislative uncertainty, however, the threat of private treble-damage suits under the Robinson-Patman Act remains. In pricing its products within the United States market, therefore, the exporter should take the requirements of that Act into account.

The Robinson-Patman Act prohibits the interstate sale of like goods at prices which discriminate between different purchasers whenever injury to competition is reasonably possible. The prohibition does not apply, however, if the seller can show that the price differences are cost justified, or resulted from the need to meet competition, or were due to changing market conditions. Since the

Supreme Court has held that *any* price difference between different purchasers of like goods constitutes a price discrimination, geographic price differences, price differences between different classes of customers, and discount schedules resulting in price differences between competing customers all raise questions under the Act.[18] To summarize the ground rules for establishing lawful geographic price differences and volume discounts:

The Act does not forbid all geographic price differences, but only those which may injure competition. The typical geographic price discrimination case in which injury is found involves a large, financially powerful seller who has made a drastic price reduction — usually below cost — limited to a particular area and aimed at a smaller competitor.[19] A basic ground rule in setting different prices for different areas of the United States, then, is to be guided by market price levels and transportation costs and to avoid below-cost reductions for predatory purposes.

Volume or quantity discount schedules usually produce price discriminations between competing customers. Sellers of standardized commodities sold for resale are the most vulnerable defendants in lawsuits involving discrimination of this kind. In such lawsuits, the so-called *Morton Salt* doctrine applies and competitive injury will be inferred whenever the discrimination is of long duration, is substantial in relation to customers' profit margins, and keen competition exists between favored and unfavored customers in the resale of the commodity.[20] The best insurance against possible Robinson-Patman liability for the seller who employs discount schedules is a cost analysis showing that the different discount brackets are cost justified. That is, the discount brackets are shown to reflect differences in the cost of manufacture, sale or delivery resulting from different methods or quantities of sale or delivery.

The Robinson-Patman Act also prohibits sellers from paying brokerage commissions or discounts in lieu of brokerage to buyers or their agents (a seller may lawfully pay such commissions only to his own agent), and requires sellers who furnish promotional allowances or services to make them available on proportionally equal terms to all competing customers.

Extent to Which the Exporter Can Control Distribution within the United States

For many years, the trend of the decisions has been to lessen the degree of control a seller can lawfully exercise over the distribution of its products. Nevertheless, some control can still be exercised, and the remainder of this paper is devoted to comment on the legal status of the following restrictive distribution practices: the appointment of exclusive distributors; the placing of territorial and customer restrictions on distributors and dealers; the inclusion of requirements and tying clauses in distribution agreements; and refusals to deal with, and terminations of, distributors and dealers.

Exclusive Distributorships

A seller's right to appoint exclusive distributors was affirmed in *United States v. Arnold Schwinn & Co.*, where the Supreme Court stated, "[I]f nothing more is involved than vertical 'confinement' of the manufacturer's own sales of the merchandise to selected dealers, and if competitive products are readily available to others, the restriction, on these facts alone, would not violate the Sherman Act."[21] What the rule permits is a self-imposed limitation by the manufacturer as to the parties to whom he will sell.

If monopolization is neither intended nor threatened, a single exclusive distributor may be appointed for the entire United States. The appointment of a sole representative in the United States by an English distiller of Scotch whiskey was recently upheld under these conditions.[22]

It is important to remember, especially where distribution is through multiple distributors, each having an exclusive territory, that the manufacturer must act unilaterally. Where the appointment of exclusive distributors is induced solely or primarily by the distributors,[23] or where existing distributors are allowed to veto the appointment of new distributors,[24] there may be an unlawful horizontal restraint.

Territorial and Customer Restrictions on Distributors and Dealers

A manufacturer's ability lawfully to impose territorial or customer limitations on distributors or dealers depends on the nature of its transactions with them. Such restrictions may not be imposed on distributors or dealers to whom the manufacturer *sells* its products. In the *Schwinn* case the Supreme Court held, "Under the Sherman Act, it is unreasonable without more for a manufacturer to seek to restrict and confine areas or persons with whom an article may be traded after the manufacturer has parted with dominion over it."

Territorial and customer restrictions may be imposed on distributors or dealers, however, wherever the manufacturer deals with them under agency or consignment arrangements. But as stated in the *Schwinn* decision, in cases where the manufacturer retains title, dominion and risk with respect to the product, and the role of the distributor or dealer is not distinguishable from that of an agent or salesman, territorial and customer restrictions are unlawful only if they are "unreasonably" restrictive of competition, Don't let anyone tell you that the law is concerned only with the substance and not with the form of a transaction!

Several courts have interpreted *Schwinn's* holding of *per se* illegality for territorial and customer *resale* restrictions as being limited to instances where the seller "firmly and resolutely" enforces the restriction.[25] However, the rationale of these decisions has been questioned by some authorities, and I would not advise reliance upon them. A company exporting to the United States should not include territorial or customer restrictions in distributorship or dealer agreements at all.

It should be noted, however, that some exceptions to the general rule against territorial and customer resale restrictions have been recognized by the courts.[26] Also, several alternatives to an outright territorial restriction, such as the "area of primary responsibility" clause and the "dealer location" clause, have received judicial sanction.[27]

The courts have been fairly tolerant of requirements contracts and they may be lawfully employed in various circumstances. The Supreme Court has said that "a requirement contract may escape censure if only a small share of the market is involved, if the purpose of the agreement is to insure to the customer a sufficient supply of a commodity vital to the customer's trade or to insure to the supplier a market for his output and if there is no trend toward concentration in the industry."[28]

Requirements contracts generally are tested under the standards of Section 3 of the Clayton Act, which expressly applies to exclusive dealing types of arrangements capable of lessening competition.[29] In *Tampa Electric Co. v. Nashville Coal Co.*, the Supreme Court held that in order for such contracts to violate Section 3, they must substantially foreclose competition in the relevant market.[30] The Court made it clear that the determination of this issue is not to be based solely on the dollar volume of sales made under the contracts, but is to involve an assessment of the effect of the contracts on competition in the market and consideration of the business reasons that gave rise to them. Many requirements contracts will stand up under this test.

Requirements contracts are more likely to be found unlawful when tested under the lesser standards of Section 5 of the Federal Trade Commission Act. If they involve a substantial seller and a large number of dealers, the Federal Trade Commission may find their use to be an unfair method of competition without even inquiring as to their effect on competition.[31]

In contrast to their generally lenient treatment of requirements contracts, the courts have been very severe in their treatment of tying arrangements. By "tying arrangement" I mean the sale or lease of one item – the tying item – on condition that a second and separate item – the tied item – be purchased or leased. Section 3 of the Clayton Act applies to tying arrangements, but only to those involving sales or leases of commodities. Section 1 of the Sherman Act, not being so limited in scope, has been applied when the tying item consisted of such noncommodities as the extension of credit, contracts for the sale or lease of land, advertising space in newspapers, and trademark licenses.[32]

Asserting on numerous occasions that tying arrangements "serve hardly any purpose beyond the suppression of competition," the Supreme Court has declared them to be illegal *per se* if they meet certain standards under Section 1 of the Sherman Act or certain lesser standards under Section 3 of the Clayton Act.[33] These standards are automatically met whenever the tying item is patented or copyrighted, or it is a distinctive trademark enjoying unique public acceptance, and the tying arrangement forecloses a "not insubstantial" amount of commerce.

Even though a tie-in is not embodied in a written agreement, it can be found from a course of conduct. In a recent private treble-damage suit against Volkswagenwerk, it was shown that VW required dealers to promote VW parts – including air conditioners, that dealers found it difficult to handle more than one line of air conditioners, and that VW had pressured dealers to carry only one line. Based on this showing, the court ruled that there was sufficient evidence upon which a jury could find Section 1, Sherman Act and Section 3, Clayton Act violations.[34]

Tying arrangements sometimes will be upheld where the second item must meet certain standards and duplication of the item is impracticable. If duplication is practicable, however, the supplier must furnish the buyer with specifications so that he can, if he wishes, obtain the second item from a supplier of his own choice.

Refusals to Deal with, and Terminations of, Distributors and Dealers

The law recognizes the right of the individual manufacturer to select its own customers, and to refuse to deal with anyone, providing the refusal to deal is not in furtherance of a monopolistic purpose (*Colgate* doctrine). Collective refusals to deal, however, are illegal *per se*.[35] Not even the elimination of competitive abuses or unethical practices will justify them.[36]

Despite the manufacturer's right of refusal to deal, terminations of distributor and dealer franchises have been a major source of antitrust litigation. The typical situation involves the transfer of an exclusive franchise from the existing distributor to a new distributor. Ordinarily, the manufacturer will first contract with the new distributor and then terminate the existing franchise. Recognizing that this is the only practicable way in which an exclusive franchise can be transferred, the courts have almost uniformly refused to consider such a termination as amounting to an unlawful concerted refusal to deal, even if as a result of the termination the former distributor's business has been seriously damaged.[37]

Because every termination of a distributor or dealer raises the specter of a treble-damage suit, the exporter would be well advised to make a record of legitimate business reasons for every such termination. In a recent suit by a former beer distributor against the brewer, the court stated that no anticompetitive intent could be inferred from the act of termination in light of the legitimate business reasons which had been shown. These included the poor condition of the distributor's warehouse, the inadequacy of its transportation equipment, and the fewer number of salesmen and drivers it had as compared to the new distributor.[38]

Such legitimate business reasons *must* exist in terminating an automobile dealer franchise, since under the "Automobile Dealers Day in Court Act" the failure of an automobile manufacturer to exercise "good faith" in canceling or not renewing such a franchise is legally actionable.[39] In a number of states there are so-called "franchise" statutes which require "good cause" for the termination of a franchise and, in some cases, for the termination of a dealer in a nonfranchise situation as well.

[1] See *United States v. Container Corp.*, 393 U.S. 333, 337 (1969).

[2] See *FTC v. Brown Shoe Co.*, 384 U.S. 321 (1966).

[3] *United States v. Trenton Potteries Co.*, 273 U.S. at 397-398 (1927).

[4] 310 U.S. 223 (1940).

[5] See, *e.g., Esco Corp. v. United States*, 340 F.2d 1000, 1006-1007 (9th Cir. 1965).

[6] 2 Trade Reg. Rep. ¶6061.

[7] *Dr. Miles Medical Co. v. John D. Park & Sons*, 220 U.S. 373 (1911).

[8] *FTC v. Beech-Nut Packing Co.*, 257 U.S. 441 (1922).

[9] *Albrecht v. Herald Co.*, 390 U.S. 145 (1968).

[10] *Simpson v. Union Oil Co.*, 377 U.S. 949 (1964).

[11] *Pearl Brewing Co. v. Anheuser-Busch, Inc.*, 339 F. Supp. 945 (S.D. Tex. 1972).

[12] *Greene v. General Foods Corp.*, 517 F.2d 635 (5th Cir. 1975).

[13] *United States v. Colgate & Co.*, 250 U.S. 300-307 (1919).

[14] *United States v. Parke, Davis & Co.*, 362 U.S. 29, 43-45. (1960).

[15] Antidumping Act of 1921, 19 U.S.C. §160 *et seq., as amended,* Trade Act of 1974, Ch. 2, §321, 2 U.S. Code Cong. & Ad. News at 2367 (Jan. 3, 1975) (provides an administrative remedy which requires a dumping duty when injury is found); Section 801 of the Revenue Act of 1916, 15 U.S.C. §72 (provides for criminal prosecutions by the government and treble-damage suits by injured domestic competitors).

[16] See "Escalating Conflict—Protectionist Feuds, Aggravated by Slump, Threaten a Trade War—Common Market Complains of U.S. Import Inquiries; Geneva Talks Jeopardized," *The Wall Street Journal,* Oct. 15, 1975.

[17] 15 U.S.C. §13(a)-(f).

[18] *FTC v. Anheuser-Busch, Inc.*, 363 U.S. 536, 545 (1960).

[19] See, *e.g., Moore v. Mead's Fine Bread Co.*, 348 U.S. 115 (1954).

[20] *FTC v. Morton Salt Co.*, 334 U.S. 37 (1948).

[21] 388 U.S. 376 (1967).

[22] *Paddington Corp. v. Major Brands, Inc.*, 359 F. Supp. 1244 (W.D. Okla. 1973).

[23] *Fontana Aviation, Inc. v. Beech Aircraft Corp.*, 432 F.2d 1080, 1085 (7th Cir.), *cert. denied,* 401 U.S. 923 (1971).

[24] *American Motor Inns, Inc. v. Holiday Inns, Inc.*, 365 F. Supp. 1073, 1085-1091 (D.N.J. 1973), *aff'd. in part, rev'd. in part and remanded,* 5 Trade Reg. Rep. ¶60,390 (3d Cir., June 30, 1975).

[25] See, *e.g., Janel Sales Corp. v. Lanvin Parfums, Inc.*, 396 F.2d 398, 406-407 (2d Cir.), *cert. denied,* 393 U.S. 938 (1968); *Colorado Pump & Supply Co. v. Febco, Inc.*, 472 F.2d 637, 639-640 (10th Cir.), *cert. denied,* 411 U.S. 987 (1973).

[26] See, *e.g., Tripoli Co. v. Wella Corp.*, 425 F.2d 932 (3d Cir.), *cert. denied,* 400 U.S. 831 (1970) (need to protect public from injury, and manufacturer from product liability claims, justified restricting distributors' resales of hazardous hair care product to professional beauticians).

[27] For court decrees approving use of area of primary responsibility clauses in franchise agreements, see, *e.g., United States v. Topco Associates, Inc.*, 1973 Trade Cas. ¶74,391 (N.D. Ill.), *aff'd.,* 414 U.S. 801 (1973); *United States v. Arnold Schwinn & Co.*, 1968 Trade Cas. ¶72,480 (N.D. Ill.). For court decisions upholding lawfulness of dealer location clauses, see, *e.g., Salco Corp. v. General Motors Corp.*, 517 F.2d 567 (10th Cir. 1975); *Kaiser v. General Motors Corp.*, 396 F. Supp. 33 (E.D. Pa. 1975).

[28] *Brown Shoe Co. v. United States*, 370 U.S. 294, 330 (1962).

[29] 15 U.S.C. §14.

[30] 365 U.S. 320 (1961).

[31] *FTC v. Brown Shoe Co.*, 384 U.S. 316, 322 (1966).

[32] *Fortner Enterprises, Inc. v. United States Steel Corp.*, 394 U.S. 495 (1969) (extension of credit); *Northern Pac. Ry. v. United States*, 356 U.S. 1 (1958) (contracts for sale or lease of land); *Times-Picayune Publishing Co. v. United States*, 345 U.S. 594 (1953) (advertising space); and *Siegel v. Chicken Delight, Inc.*, 448 F.2d 43 (9th Cir. 1971), *cert. denied,* 405 U.S. 955 (1972) (trademark licenses).

[33] *Standard Oil Co. v. United States,* 337 U.S. 293, 305-306 (1949).

[34] *Heatransfer Corp. v. Volkswagenwerk A.G.,* 1975 Trade Cas. ¶60,306 (S.D. Tex., Sept. 30, 1974).

[35] *Klor's Inc. v. Broadway-Hale Stores, Inc.,* 359 U.S. 207 (1959).

[36] See, *e.g., Fashion Originators' Guild of America, Inc. v. FTC,* 312 U.S. 457 (1941).

[37] See, *e.g., Burdett Sound, Inc. v. Altec Corp.,* 1975-2 Trade Cas. ¶60,404 at 66,775 (5th Cir., July 21, 1975) and cases cited in opinion.

[38] *John Lenore & Co. v. Olympia Brewing Co.,* 1975-2 Trade Cas. ¶60,505 (S.D. Cal., June 5, 1975).

[39] Automobile Dealers Day in Court Act, 15 U.S.C. §1221-1225.

The United States – Land of Licensing Opportunity

James H. Wallace, Jr. *

GOVERNMENT INTERFERENCE with licensing is perhaps today's greatest obstacle to efficient and profitable transfer of technology and other proprietary rights. Examples of particularly bothersome regulations in effect in many countries include registration requirements under which an agreement cannot go into effect until it has been filed and approved by government bureaucracy. Royalty limitations prohibiting the charging of license fees above a specified low rate and currency restrictions providing that the royalties are to be paid in local soft currencies are impediments to licensing in various Latin American countries. Forfeiture regulations, which provide that a licensee owns the licenser's trademark after the first few years of a license, are now in effect in Argentina. And prohibitions against normal licensing restrictions such as fields of use and territorial limitations are becoming widespread in the developing countries. These and countless other obstacles are thorns in the side of aggressive international licensers.[1]

Recent U.S. Government Actions Emphasize the Importance of Complying with United States Antitrust Laws

The United States is far more hospitable to licensing than most countries. But, to be sure, we have our rules of the game – imposed by our antitrust and other laws. Failure to observe these legal requirements can result in troublesome legal proceedings. Recent suits by the Justice Department's Antitrust Division have challenged the licensing practices of a number of foreign companies. For example, in the *Glaxo* case, the government challenged the so-called bulk licensing restrictions imposed by two giant United Kingdom firms on their United States licensees.[2] The *Ampicillin* case attacks patent procurement and enforcement practices of a large United Kingdom drug company.[3]

Similarly, *United States v. Farbenfabriken Bayer, A.G.* challenged field-of-use restrictions on resale imposed on over 100 American companies by the German defendant.[4] Patent licensing practices of another German patentee in the industrial chemical area are challenged in *United States v. Ziegler*.[5] And of course, the *Westinghouse-Mitsubishi* case is a head-on challenge to the exclusive technology agreements between two Japanese firms and Westinghouse.[6]

But government suits are not the only problem. In addition, potential licensees who are unsuccessful in obtaining a license and potential licensers who are unable to convince infringers to take a license have interesting legal weapons in their arsenal. Civil treble-damage suits by allegedly injured parties can produce multimillion-dollar disasters such as in the television patent pool cases.[7]

Structuring the License Agreement to Minimize Antitrust Risks and Maximize Profits

From a purely profit standpoint, the ideal license might provide that the licensee cannot compete with the licenser or other licensees; that he would charge prices no lower than the licenser's prices; or that his geographical area of competition would be strictly limited. Moreover, in this hypothetical profit-maximizing case, as a condition for obtaining a license, the licensee would be required to purchase all sorts of unrelated and unpatented materials from the licenser.

However, the United States antitrust laws treat overly restrictive licensing harshly. This is not to say, however, that all licensing restrictions are to be avoided. Profit can be maximized with well-planned licensing limitations. The objective — easily stated, but often difficult to achieve — is to balance the somewhat conflicting desire to maximize restraints to increase profits with the need to minimize restraints in order to avoid antitrust risks and patent misuses.[8]

There are few hard and fast rules in this area, but there are guidelines with respect to the types of licensing practices that can be used under appropriate circumstances. Likewise, the precedents provide clues as to practices that conservative companies are well advised to avoid.

Examples of Commercially Beneficial Licensing Practices Which Can Be Used Under Appropriate Circumstances

Field-of-use limitations are quite valuable where the invention is useful in a variety of applications. For example, a new plastic might readily be molded into twenty-five-cent ashtrays and also be useful for noses on $30-million 747 jet planes. Obviously, the appropriate royalty for the ashtray would be considerably less than what the market might bear for the jet plane noses. Moreover, the patentee may wish to reserve the more lucrative jet field for himself. There is authority supporting the legality of field-of-use restrictions based on such *technological* distinctions.[9] Problems may be encountered, however, where the field-of-use restriction is in reality a *marketing* restriction. For example, "wholesale distribution only," or "finished" as opposed to "bulk" products are typical field-of-use restrictions used by pharmaceutical companies respecting the marketing of the patented product, not its ultimate end use.[10]

Domestic territorial restrictions are of obvious benefit to the patentee, but require careful analysis. The Patent Code provides that a patentee may grant "an exclusive right" under its patent "to the whole or any specified part of the United States."[11] At least one recent case indicates that this assignment statute legitimizes domestic territorial restrictions that might otherwise violate the antitrust laws.[12] Some antitrust authorities strongly disagree with this contention.[13] But since few patentees seek to take advantage of the apparent permissiveness of the statute, there has been very little litigation on the subject.[14]

International territorial limitations present still further opportunities. For example, a patentee may wish to license his patent in one country while refraining from licensing counterpart patents in other countries. Although this may well have the same effect as an explicit agreement dividing territories, the practice is believed by many to be perfectly legal since the territorial barriers are based on different statutory exclusive grants, *i.e.,* the various patents.[15] In the simple example given, this is probably correct.

The problem becomes more complex, however, in cases involving cross-licenses providing for mutually exclusive territories. Such arrangements, especially if coupled with still further restrictions, can quickly lead to situations similar to the classic cartel cases.[16] The problem becomes even more complex when the cross-licenses include provisions for the exchange of technology and patents developed in the future, such as is alleged in the government's *Westinghouse-Mitsubishi* complaint.[17] Of course, an entirely different assessment may be required if the territorial division is achieved by licensing *unpatented* know-how.[18]

In any event, international territorial limitations present challenging questions for thoughtful legal analysis. As the chief of the Antitrust Division's Foreign Commerce Section recently conceded, the old cartel cases leave a great deal of uncertainty in this area because of their complex factual situations and the presence in those cases of an aggregation of restraints.[19]

Grantbacks are provisions by which the licenser requires his licensees to convey to him rights on improvements to the invention made by the licensee. Obviously, the licenser does not want to find his products rendered obsolete in the marketplace by an innovative licensee. On the other hand, public policy and antitrust principles do not favor arrangements that discourage innovation. A narrowly drawn, reasonable grantback provision is a judicially recognized compromise.[20] But overly broad grantbacks can create considerable antitrust risk. Factors to be considered in evaluating the legality of a particular grantback include whether the grantback provision assigns the entire improvement rights or is a mere nonexclusive license to the patentee; whether there are a number of licenses containing provisions whereby the patentee can funnel back everybody's improvements to himself; whether the patentee will pay a royalty to the licensee developing the improvement; whether the licenser competes with the licensee; and whether other restrictions are in the agreement.[21]

Examples of Commercially Beneficial Licensing Practices Which May Raise Antitrust Problems in Certain Circumstances

Price limitations in patent agreements which force the licensee to sell at the same price as the patentee can raise serious antitrust problems, despite the Supreme Court's famous 1926 *General Electric* ruling,[22] and despite recent cases indicating possible areas of permissive price fixing in licenses.[23] The patentee's competitive advantage gained from not having royalty burdens and from being first in the field should usually give him a sufficient competitive edge so that such price fixing is not necessary even if it is arguably legal.

Tie-ins in licenses require the licensee to make purchases from the patentee as a condition to getting the license. "Tie-ins" are frequently held illegal *per se* under the antitrust laws. But there are situations where even this practice may be justified. For example, the *Jerrold* case[24] recognized that entry into a new technological field might justify tie-in restrictions *for a limited time*.[25] Interesting legal problems akin to tie-ins are presented when a licenser has patents, know-how and trademarks all related to the same subject matter.

Miscellaneous other practices can raise antitrust problems under certain circumstances. Examples include resale problems,[26] exclusive dealing requirements,[27] improper procurement and enforcement of the patents,[28] and agreements tending to inhibit further licensing, such as "semi-exclusive licenses."[29] Moreover, the manner in which a licensee's royalties are calculated can raise a full spectrum of antitrust problems.[30]

Conclusion

Whatever the particular licensing limitation may be, questions regarding its legality should *not* be answered in the abstract, but should be subjected to a sophisticated factual and legal analysis. Most of the antitrust rules have exceptions.[31] Likewise, conduct which alone is legal can become part of an overall antitrust violation in the context of a particular factual situation.[32]

[1]See generally E.M. Aguilar, *Changing Attitudes and Perspectives in Developing Countries Regarding Technology Licensing, les* Nouvelles (special ed. June 1972), at 28, 31; E.M. Aguilar, *Two Years with Mexican Law,* 10 *les* Nouvelles 135 (1975); A. Delgado, *Analysis of Laws of Technology Transfer,* 10 *les* Nouvelles 137, 138-39 (1975); F.M. Lacey, *Technology and Industrial Property Licensing in Latin America,* 6 International Lawyer 388 (1972); R.D. Manahan, *Legislation Affecting Licensing,* 10 *les* Nouvelles 120, 121 (1975); H.B. Thomsen, *Legal Restraints on Licensing,* 10 *les* Nouvelles 6, 43 (1975).

[2]*United States v. Glaxo Group Ltd.,* 410 U.S. 52 (1973). See also *United States v. Ciba Corp.,* Civil No. 791-69 (D.N.J., Complaint filed July 9, 1969); *United States v. Ciba Corp. and CPC Int'l Inc.,* Civil No. 792-69 (D.N.J., Complaint filed July 9, 1969); and *United States v. Fisons Ltd.,* Civil No. 69 C 1530 (N.D. Ill., Complaint filed July 23, 1969).

[3]*United States v. Bristol-Myers Co.,* Civil No. 822-70 (D.D.C., Complaint filed March 19, 1970); see also *In re Ampicillin Antitrust Litigation,* 55 F.R.D. 269 (D.D.C. 1972).

[4]Civil No. 586-68 (D.D.C., Complaint filed March 7, 1968); see also *United States v. Farbenfabriken Bayer A.G.,* 1969 Trade Cas. ¶72,918 (D.D.C.) (consent decree).

[5]Civil No. 1255-70 (D.D.C., Complaint filed April 24, 1970).

[6]*United States v. Westinghouse Elec. Corp., Mitsubishi Elec. Corp., and Mitsubishi Heavy Indus., Ltd.,* Civil No. C 70-852-SAW (N.D. Cal., Complaint filed April 22, 1970).

[7]*Zenith Radio Corp. v. Hazeltine Research, Inc.,* 395 U.S. 100, 106 (1969), *modified,* 401 U.S. 321 (1971) ($35 million damages). See also *West Virginia v. Chas. Pfizer & Co.,* 314 F. Supp. 710 (S.D.N.Y. 1970), aff'd, 440 F.2d 1079 (2d Cir. 1971), *cert. denied,* 404 U.S. 871 (1971) (66 plaintiffs settled for $100 million).

[8] The patent "misuse" doctrine provides a defense to a patent infringement action even if the patentee's conduct falls short of an actual antitrust violation. See generally J.H. Wallace, *Proper Use of the Patent Misuse Doctrine — An Antitrust Defense to Patent Infringement Actions in Need of Rational Reform*, 26 Mercer L. Rev. 813 (1975).

[9] See generally *General Talking Pictures Corp. v. Western Elec. Co.*, 304 U.S. 175 (1938); W. F. Baxter, *Legal Restrictions on Exploitation of the Patent Monopoly: An Economic Analysis*, 76 Yale L. J. 267, 339-46 (1966); G. R. Gibbons, Field Restrictions in Patent *Transactions: Economic Discrimination and Restraint of Competition*, 66 Colum. L. Rev. 423 (1966); Address by Richard H. Stern before Licensing Executives Society in New York City, April 5, 1967; D. Turner, *The Patent System and Competitive Policy*, 44 N.Y.U. L. Rev. 450, 470-72 (1969); Remarks of Bruce B. Wilson before the Fourth New England Antitrust Conference, Boston, Mass., Nov. 6, 1970.

[10] Restrictions on resale of bulk pharmaceuticals were ruled illegal in the circumstances of *United States v. Glaxo Group Ltd.*, 302 F. Supp. 1 (D.D.C. 1969), *modified*, 410 U.S. 52 (1973). Additional clarification of the legality of marketing restrictions in licensing may evolve from the forthcoming trial in *United States v. Ciba Corp.*, Civil No. 791-69 (D.N.J., Complaint filed July 9, 1969).

[11] 35 U.S.C. § 261 (1970).

[12] See *Dunlop Co. v. Kelsey-Hayes Co.*, 484 F.2d 407, 417-18 (6th Cir. 1973), *cert. denied*, 415 U.S. 917 (1974), which held that although a patentee's granting of exclusive licenses to different parties in several countries "might limit commerce in the patented device," this was "purely incidental" and "cannot be characterized as true horizontal agreements dividing markets," but are "merely territorial licenses granted by a patentee such as are permitted by 35 U.S.C. § 261."

[13] W.F. Baxter, *Legal Restrictions on Exploitation of the Patent Monopoly: An Economic Analysis*, 76 Yale L.J. 267, 347-52 (1966); G.R. Gibbons, *Domestic Territorial Restrictions in Patent Transactions and the Antitrust Laws*, 34 Geo. Wash. L. Rev. 893 (1966); D. Turner, *The Patent System and Competitive Policy*, 44 N.Y.U. L. Rev. 450, 474-76 (1969).

[14] See ABA *Antitrust Law Developments*, Ch. 9, *Patent-Antitrust Problems*, at 349 (1975).

[15] R.H. Stern, *The Antitrust Status of Territorial Limitations in International Licensing*, 14 Idea 580 (1970-71); Remarks of Bruce B. Wilson before the Fourth New England Antitrust Conference, Boston, Mass., Nov. 6, 1970. See also *Dunlop Co. v. Kelsey-Hayes Co.*, *supra* note 12.

[16] E.g., *Timken Roller Bearing Co. v. United States*, 341 U.S. 593 (1951); *United States v. National Lead Co.*, 63 F. Supp. 513 (S.D.N.Y. 1945), *aff'd*, 332 U.S. 319 (1947).

[17] *United States v. Westinghouse Elec. Corp., Mitsubishi Elec. Corp., and Mitsubishi Heavy Indus., Ltd.*, Civil No. C 70-852-SAW (N.D. Cal., Complaint filed April 22, 1970).

[18] R.H. Stern, *The Antitrust Status of Territorial Limitations in International Licensing*, 14 Idea 580, 589-90 (1970-71).

[19] Address by Joel Davidow before the American Bar Association Antitrust Section, Honolulu, Hawaii, August 13, 1974, 43 ABA Antitrust L.J. (1975).

[20] Cf. *Transparent-Wrap Mach. Corp. v. Stokes & Smith Co.*, 329 U.S. 637 (1947). See generally P.G. Chevigny, *The Validity of Grant-Back Agreements Under the Antitrust Laws*, 34 Fordham L. Rev. 569 (1966).

[21] See Chevigny, *supra* note 20. See also *United States v. Wisconsin Alumni Research Foundation*, 1970 Trade Cas. ¶ 73,015 (W.D. Wis.) (consent decree).

[22] *United States v. General Elec. Co.*, 272 U.S. 476 (1926). See generally G.R. Gibbons, *Price Fixing in Patent Licenses and the Antitrust Laws*, 51 Va. L. Rev. 273 (1965).

[23] See e.g., *Congoleum Indus. v. Armstrong Cork Co.*, 366 F. Supp. 220, 228-31 (E.D. Pa. 1973), *aff'd, 510 F.2d 334 (3d Cir. 1975)*, cert. denied, 43 U.S.L.W. 3625 (May 27, 1975) (license provision set rate licensee could charge sublicensees).

[24] *United States v. Jerrold Electronics Corp.*, 187 F. Supp. 545 (E.D. Pa. 1960), *aff'd per curiam*, 365 U.S. 567 (1961); see also *Jack Winter, Inc. v. Koratron Co.*, 375 F. Supp. 1 (N.D. Cal. 1974); *Falls Church Bratwursthaus, Inc. v. Bratwursthaus Management Corp.*, 354 F. Supp. 1237 (E.D. Va. 1973); Address by Richard H. Stern before Licensing Executives Society in New York City, April 5, 1967.

[25] See also *Dehydrating Process Co. v. A.O. Smith Corp.*, 292 F.2d 653 (1st Cir.), *cert. denied*, 368 U.S. 931 (1961) (refusal to sell patented devices unless installed in seller's

container not illegal "tie-in" where restriction was motivated by quality control considerations).

[26] Compare *United States v. Glaxo Group Ltd.*, 302 F. Supp. 1 (D.D.C. 1969), *modified*, 410 U.S. 52 (1973), with *Tripoli Co. v. Wella Corp.*, 425 F.2d 932 (3d Cir.), *cert. denied*, 400 U.S. 831 (1970).

[27] *E.g., Berlenbach v. Anderson & Thompson Ski Co.*, 329 F.2d 782 (9th Cir.), *cert. denied*, 379 U.S. 830 (1964).

[28] See ABA *Antitrust Law Developments*, Ch. 9, *Patent-Antitrust Problems*, at 331-35 (1975).

[29] See *Recent Government Patent Antitrust Suits*, Address by Richard H. Stern before Western Corporate Patent Seminar, Colorado Springs, Colo., September 30, 1968.

[30] See, *e.g., LaPeyre v. FTC*, 366 F.2d 117 (5th Cir. 1966); see generally ABA *Antitrust Law Developments*, Ch. 9, *Patent-Antitrust Problems*, at 342-44 (1975).

[31] See *United States v. Jerrold Electronics Corp.*, 187 F. Supp. 545 (E.D. Pa. 1960), *aff'd per curiam*, 365 U.S. 567 (1961); *Dehydrating Process Co. v. A.O. Smith Corp.*, 292 F.2d 653 (1st Cir.), *cert. denied*, 368 U.S. 931 (1961); and Department of Justice Luncheon Speech, *Law on Licensing Practices: Myth or Reality or Straight Talk from "Alice in Wonderland,"* Remarks by Bruce B. Wilson before the American Patent Law Association, Washington, D.C., Jan. 21, 1975 at 11-13.

[32] *Continental Ore Co. v. Union Carbide & Carbon Corp.*, 370 U.S. 690 (1962).

An Overview of the Direction of U.S. Antitrust Law — Problems of the Multinational —1

Allen C. Holmes *

THIS PAPER IS an overview of the direction in which I see antitrust policy moving in the United States, particularly as it relates to multinational corporations and their problems. I would emphasize that this overview is bound to be partial. It reflects the perspective of a private practitioner who, over a period of years, has had considerable exposure to those responsible for policymaking within the Antitrust Division, particularly through discussions concerning specific antitrust problems.

In the United States we have the rather anomalous situation of two separate antitrust enforcement agencies with overlapping, but only partially overlapping, responsibilities. I think it is fair to say that the Antitrust Division has tended to focus on problems involving international transactions to a much greater extent than has the Federal Trade Commission. But, as Paul Victor has suggested (see pages 45 to 54), the Federal Trade Commission has been very active in some areas of international commerce, such as mergers, and acquisitions. I propose to focus to a major degree on the activities of the Antitrust Division.

The Antitrust Division is not the monolithic structure that it might appear to be. It is a highly competent bureaucracy which continues on, no matter what administration is in power. In addition to the basic bureaucracy, the Division has a politically appointed leadership, headed by the Assistant Attorney General of the United States in charge of the Antitrust Division, who holds office at the pleasure of the administration in power and, to some degree at least, reflects the policies and decisions of the elected executive. Apart from the differences of view which arise between an ongoing bureaucracy and an appointed staff, there are all of the usual wide variances in view that one might expect among a group of very able, generally hardworking, and intensely interested lawyers. There are activists who want to test the outer reaches of the law, and there are more conservative lawyers. With all this said, I think it is still fair to say that there are certain trends developing in the administration of the antitrust laws by the Department of Justice that are worth noting and are sufficiently definitive to be identified and evaluated.

In the post-World War II period, the American economy experienced an enormous expansion. While I do not believe there was a significant increase in concentration of industry during that period, there was a very large increase in the volume of assets held by the major corporations in the United States. Total productive capital has expanded enormously in the last 30 years. During this

---

*Partner in law firm of Jones, Day, Reavis & Pogue, Cleveland, Ohio.

period, the Antitrust Division assumed a critical role in preserving the character and extent of the competitive activity in our economy.

The courts, and particularly the Supreme Court under Chief Justice Warren, urged the Antitrust Division to take a more and more expansive view of the powers conferred upon the government by the antitrust laws to control and guide business activities, particularly mergers and acquisitions. Antitrust law became the ultimate arbitrator of business conduct. Whatever other social, economic or political values might be involved in various business transactions, the ultimate determinant of the propriety of business conduct became the antitrust laws and the constraints which the courts read into the very general language of the antitrust statutes. Moreover, it became clear that if any probable, or even possible, antitrust violation could be found, this fact alone was enough to prohibit the transaction even though there might be other procompetitive aspects present.[1]

Evolving Antitrust Policy

Beginning in the 1970's, a new set of social concerns, goals and problems captured the attention of the public, the Congress, the Executive, and the Courts. The quality of life became ever more significant. Development of sources of energy suddenly became of paramount importance. The need to obtain sources or alternatives for many basic raw materials became critical. Development of policies in these various areas has inevitably brought about legislative, executive and administrative attitudes and actions which, at the very least, now require a new approach to the harmonization of antitrust policy with these new and significant social, economic and political objectives.

The development of, and concern with, these aspects of our economic world has not led to any abatement of antitrust enforcement activities in the United States, but it has forced the Antitrust Division to reconsider how antitrust policy can be integrated with these other government policies. The Antitrust Division is beginning to recognize that these other policies are important to the preservation of a vigorous democratic society and may mandate domestic policies inconsistent with a total free market economy of the type the antitrust laws are thought by the Department of Justice to require.

Paralleling these domestic developments have been a group of significant developments in the international economy. World trade has grown enormously. Multinational corporations have grown even more rapidly. These corporations have attained positions of enormous significance in the development of the world's natural resources, in the movement of technologies from the developed to the developing countries, and in the internationalization of trade. Not surprisingly, these corporations have been the object of intense criticism which, in my view, is unjustified to a major degree. In this connection I call your attention to a report by a group of eminent persons assessing the impact of multinational corporations on development and on international relations.[2] I find the report peculiarly unbalanced. On the other hand, many of the papers in the recently published volume edited by George Ball ably describe the affirmative contributions of the multinational corporations.[3]

Another aspect of the changing international economic order has been the enormous expansion of governments' role in the private economy through minority or majority ownership of private companies. In addition, there are increasing demands by the developing countries for policies concerned primarily with considerations of equity rather than with the more traditional concerns of the efficient allocation of scarce resources.

All of these complex issues have had a substantial impact upon the direction of the thinking of those having responsibility for antitrust administration in the Department of Justice. The reevaluation that is in progress within the Department has, I believe, a great significance for the multinational corporations and for our international commerce. I see a vastly reduced effort to expand the role of structuralist antitrust theory. This would represent a significant change of direction. Encouraged by the courts and driven by Congress, the Antitrust Division had for a considerable period immediately prior to the last two years been pressing on the courts the validity of economic theories concerning concentration and the relationship between increasing industrial concentration and such problems as the low rate of investment, high levels of unemployment, the declining level of production of goods and services, and high interest rates. These theories were premised to a major degree on the presence of a particular economic structure without significant reference to the actual activities of the institutions which are part of that structure. Now, however, the drive to persuade courts to accept structuralist analyses seems to be in the process of being greatly tempered.

The new focus of the Antitrust Division is to introduce free market principles into many segments of the domestic and international economies where there had been precious little competition of the type found in a truly free market. Examples of this abound. The International Shipping Conference's agreements on pricing structures are being challenged, notwithstanding the degree of legislative immunity. The Department is aggressively seeking greater competition in air transportation, primarily in the domestic area but also in international traffic. In this regard the Department has supported nonscheduled air carriers and applied greater and greater pressure to the Civil Aeronautics Board in connection with its too ready acceptance of International Air Transportation Authority price structures. Competition in international communications has also been a significant objective of the Antitrust Division as overseer of the federal regulatory agencies' activities.

Domestically the Department of Justice has launched investigations concerning insurance; is vigorously pushing its efforts to secure repeal of federal fair trade laws; i.e., those laws permitting the fixing of resale prices by manufacturers or distributors;[4] and is encouraging repeal of state-enacted fair trade laws. In this area the United States is just now catching up with the position that has been taken for some time by various of the leading industrial countries of Europe. In connection with the furtherance of its efforts to broaden the areas in which the free market is truly effective, the Department is engaged in opposing antidumping petitions by private industry and is carefully scrutinizing efforts by domestic manufacturers to exclude imports on the grounds of unfair competitive practices under Section 337 of the Tariff Act of 1930.[5] It should be emphasized that the Department has always looked upon imports as significant factors in preserving truly competitive markets in many products in the United States, including the whole range of manufactured items from autos and TV and radio equipment to canned fish and plastic toys.[6]

Looked at another way, emphasis on the support of exporters to the United States, and importers into it, is part of the Department's emphasis on its role as the policeman charged with responsibility for preventing price rigidities, including price-fixing conspiracies, in the sale of manufactured goods, particularly foodstuffs. Half of the Department's budget for 1975-1976, which is in excess of $20 million, will probably be spent on ferreting out conspiracies which involve allegations of market allocation or the fixing of prices by sellers or manufacturers of goods or other products and services. I should note that multinationals and exporters to the United States are just as subject to liability for price fixing and other similar anticompetitive practices as are domestic companies.

However, if we look abroad rather than at the domestic picture, my personal experience is that the Antitrust Division of the Department of Justice is taking a fairly realistic view of international economic activity involved in the securing of basic resources needed to supply the vast flow of consumer products produced by United States manufacturers. The scarcity of basic raw materials, the demand for capital far in excess of that which is available, and the pressures of governments of underdeveloped countries for a greater participation in the goods and services produced in the world have brought about an ever-increasing tendency in most countries for government to engage in greater economic planning, resource allocation, and priority setting than would be the case in societies committed to free market economies. Consequently, competing private firms must frequently coordinate their activities and cooperate in ways that would be suspect under traditional antitrust analysis.

I believe that it is now well-known that the Justice Department has authorized, and the Sherman Act permits, necessary cooperation among American firms to deal with a foreign government or multiple foreign governments engaged in cartel activity so long as the cooperation of private United States and multinational firms does not spill over into domestic markets. Further, the Antitrust Division has usually taken the position that the antitrust laws do not prohibit any firm from complying with the demands of a foreign government even if such compliance would otherwise be offensive under our antitrust laws. It also appears that there is an increased awareness on the part of the Department of the need for joint action of questionable, borderline legality by multinational corporations in responding to veiled threats and even to "suggestions" of foreign governments when they are accompanied by examples of treatment meted out to other companies that have failed to respond to such advice.

Companies seeking to obtain the maximum cooperation of the Antitrust Division in connection with major problems, such as I have been describing, often find it desirable to keep the Division advised of activities with regard to negotiations or transactions with foreign countries. I do not mean that it is necessarily desirable in many instances, or in most cases, to seek specific affirmative approval of the course of action pursued by the company or companies involved. Requests for business review letters present many problems to those seeking them. Such requests frequently involve lengthy periods of preparation; they place the company requesting such a letter in a position where it must produce documents and data that may go far beyond the scope of the request; and the letters become public records. However, they do have the advantage that if all the conditions stated in the letter are complied with, the likelihood of any criminal action by the Department of Justice becomes almost nonexistent and the likelihood of civil action becomes remote.

Full disclosure to the Department without requesting that it take any affirmative action is frequently the most desirable course for a variety of reasons. Normally, major foreign transactions are discussed at some point with other departments of the government, particularly the State Department and, if not with our government, with the government of foreign countries. There is thus a great likelihood that the Antitrust Division will learn about the transaction from other sources, and this sequence of events can hardly be expected to please the Division. Moreover, Congress frequently learns of significant international undertakings and often seeks to ascertain what involvement the Antitrust Division has had in connection with such an undertaking. The ability of the Department to report that it is fully informed and is monitoring the situation is of great importance in protecting the administration and the parties to any such undertaking from frequently unfair censure by one or more congressional committees.

In addition, while the Antitrust Division has made very clear that it is not prepared to give informal advice, exploration of a subject through reporting processes may well provide significant guidance to antitrust advisers even though the Division has expressed no explicit opinion concerning a given subject. Further, if there does come a time when it appears that it is appropriate to seek a business review letter with respect to some aspect of a very comprehensive undertaking, the background provided through informal procedures is invaluable in giving credibility to the request for specific antitrust clearance.

Notwithstanding all that I have said concerning the increased flexibility of the Antitrust Division in its approach to antitrust matters, notwithstanding its perhaps grudging recognition of the fact that antitrust can no longer successfully assert the preeminence in policy decision making that it has recently enjoyed, notwithstanding the lessened reliance upon primary structural analysis as the underpinning for positions taken in connection with enforcement activities, the Department is still engaged in significant massive litigation affecting major multinational corporations.[7]

It is said that 15 percent of the budget of the Antitrust Division is going to the trial of the IBM case — which has major significance for all multinational corporations. Another 10 percent of its budget is devoted to the preparation of its enormous and complicated case against AT&T, which also has very great significance in the international economic scene.

Moreover, the somewhat benign thrust of recent antitrust activity is being accompanied by an ever-expanding effort on the part not only of the Antitrust Division but of the Federal Trade Commission as well to secure vast quantities of information concerning the activities of the major companies engaged in business in the United States.

Increasing Demands for Information Disclosure

The United States courts have traditionally taken a very broad view of their power to compel discovery with respect to companies, and particularly multinationals over which the courts would seem to have only a very limited basis for asserting jurisdiction. Thus the courts have insisted on the production of documents where the documents are within the control of the United States-based corporation but located outside the United States.[8] A like result has been reached where the documents were actually in the possession of a foreign corporation controlled by or controlling the United States corporation which was subject to the order of the court.[9] Likewise, the courts have had no difficulty in compelling production of documents in the control of a foreign corporation doing business within the United States whether the documents were located within the United States or outside the United States.[10] Limitation on this exercise of authority has been developed in certain of the cases, thus the courts have traditionally not insisted upon the production of documents by a foreign corporation where the foreign corporation is a government instrumentality or a private corporation controlled by a foreign government.[11] Further, a clear demonstration that production of documents might interfere with foreign policy goals of the United States has generally dissuaded courts from exercising their power to compel production.[12] Finally, some courts have recognized that it would be inappropriate to require production where to do so would clearly be inconsistent with traditional principles of comity between sovereign governments.[13]

Whether or not these restrictions will continue to give any assurance of protection of multinational or foreign corporations doing business in the United States in connection with their most private data is very doubtful. The recent massive effort of the Federal Trade Commission to secure from 450 United States corporations highly confidential information with respect to the operations of the businesses of these companies on a line-of-business basis suggests that multinational corporations, faced as they are with mounting attacks from numerous different sources, may soon face very similar demands. In this connection, the U.N. Report, which has already been mentioned, strongly urges that there be established

> "[C]ommission on multinational corporations [which] should give consideration to the convening of an expert group on international accounting standards. The task of the expert group to be to identify the information needed, determine how and in what form it should be collected, and decide how it could best be used by all concerned***"[14]

Legislation pending in the United States Senate, known as the Hart-Scott Antitrust Improvements Act of 1975 (S. 1284), if passed in its present form would represent a further expansion of the authority of the Antitrust Division to obtain information from multinational corporations. Section 703 of Title VII of that proposed legislation provides in substance that in a civil antitrust action if any party or *any persons in privy with such party* fails or refuses to respond to

76

requests for discovery or to furnish evidence or testimony on the ground that a foreign statute, order, regulation, decree or other law prohibits compliance with such court order, the court may dismiss the party's claim, strike the party's defenses, or terminate the proceeding adversely to the party. The legislative history does not give any answer to the question of when a person is in privy with a party to a civil action.

The Justice Department is opposed to the foregoing proposal. Assistant Attorney General Kauper, testifying with respect to the proposed Section 703, pointed out that it raises significant questions as to its propriety under principles of international law and comity among nations.

While dealing with this whole subject of the expanding ability of the antitrust enforcement agencies to obtain information and data concerning business activities of a company doing business in the United States, or related to a company doing business in the United States, we should note in passing the other provisions of the Hart-Scott Bill that bear on the disclosure of information to the antitrust agencies. Title II would significantly expand the prelitigation investigative powers of the Department of Justice by amending the Antitrust Civil Process Act. Title V would require premerger notification and give the antitrust authorities virtually unlimited powers to stay any transaction involving mergers or acquisitions until it was fully satisfied as to the propriety of the transaction. Of course, expanded discovery requirements imposed by the United States Federal Government are not limited to those imposed by the Antitrust Division and the Federal Trade Commission. Both the Securities and Exchange Commission and the International Trade Commission have been insisting upon increasingly extensive discovery of sensitive business information concerning international transactions.

The Legislature and the Courts

Two other facets of the antitrust environment in the United States are relevant to the situation of multinationals as competitors in the national markets of the United States. The first is Congress and congressional activity with respect to multinationals.

The Church Committee (named after its chairman), which is a subcommittee of the Foreign Relations Committee of the United States Senate, has been engaged for a considerable period of time in highly intensive scrutiny of the activities of multinational companies. The activities of that oversight committee have been extremely far-ranging and varied. For example, in the course of recent negotiations between the aluminum companies and the Government of Jamaica, supported by a newly organized bauxite cartel established by the governments of the seven principal bauxite and alumina exporting countries of the world, the Church Committee initiated an investigation that appeared to the industry to be primarily to the benefit of that cartel. Witnesses from the companies were called and examined in an apparent attempt to give credence to the claims of the Jamaica Government against the companies. One almost had the feeling that the Church Committee and the Government of Jamaica were leagued in acting against the domestic aluminum industry and the domestic customer.

Finally, attention should be directed to the changing role of the courts. During the years the Supreme Court was led by Chief Justice Warren, it had tended to prod the antitrust enforcement agency to take ever more sweeping positions with respect to the reach of the antitrust laws. The Court under Chief Justice Burger has not pursued the same policy. It has shown considerable tendency to reject a purely structuralist approach to mergers and acquisitions.[15] Further, the Court has emphasized that there must be a balance between antitrust policy and other regulatory legislation.[16]

I do not see these cases as indicating that the Court is about to turn its back on vigorous antitrust enforcement activities. Rather, I see this Court as being concerned with what Dr. Bock has so aptly termed "realism." Facts are again going to have considerable significance in the disposition of antitrust litigation. This means that the realities of international commerce, and of governmental interference in the marketplace, are going to be taken into account; however, I am satisfied that the present Court is as committed to a free market economy as was the Warren Court, but with a pragmatism and a willingness to examine facts that were not characteristic of the Court in the 1950's and 1960's.

In sum, I see the present policy of the Antitrust Division committed to a world in which international trade is as free as possible. Increasing encouragement to entry by multinationals into our domestic markets — both through the sale of goods and the investment of capital — can be expected. Whether these policies will be pursued by the administration in power after the 1976 Presidential election is anyone's guess, but I would hazard that the trends we are now observing have substantial momentum and the policies that I have described should continue in their present direction.

---

[1] *United States v. Philadelphia National Bank,* 374 U.S. 321 (1963) "We are clear, however, that a merger the effect of which 'may be substantially to lessen competition' is not saved because, on some ultimate reckoning of social or economic debits and credits, it may be deemed beneficial."

[2] *The Impact of Multinational Corporations on Development and on International Relations* (A United Nations Publication, 1974).

[3] George Ball, ed., *Global Companies, The Political Economy of World Business* (Prentice-Hall, Inc., 1975).

[4] On December 12, 1975, President Ford signed a bill which in effect repealed these laws.

[5] See H. Applebaum, "The Antidumping Laws — Impact on the Competitive Process," 43 *Antitrust L.J.* 590; P. LaRue, "Section 337 of the 1930 Tariff Act and Its Section 5 FTC Act Counterpart," 43 *Antitrust L.J.* 608 (1974).

[6] See speech by Donald I. Baker, BNA *Antitrust & Trade Regulation Report,* No. 640, November 27, 1973, E1-E4.

[7] See, *e.g., United States v. International Business Machine Corp.,* Civ. No. 69 Civ. 200 (S.D.N.Y., filed 1/17/69); *United States v. American Telephone & Telegraph Co.,* No. 74-1698 (D.D.C., filed 11/20/74); *United States v. Goodyear Tire & Rubber Co.,* Civ. No. C-73-836 (N.D. Ohio, filed 8/9/73); *United States v. Firestone Tire & Rubber Co.,* Civ. No. C-73-835 (N.D. Ohio, filed 8/9/73).

[8]See *In the Matter of Grand Jury Investigation of the Shipping Industry,* 186 F. Supp. 298 (D.D.C. 1960), even where production of such documents is contrary to a foreign law and might subject the corporation to civil liability. See *United States v. First National City Bank,* 396 F.2d 897 (2d Cir. 1968).

[9]See *In re Investigation of World Arrangements with Relation to the Production, Transportation, Refining and Distribution of Petroleum,* 1952 *Trade Cases,* Par. 67,358 (D.D.C.) (foreign subsidiary); *In the Matter of Electric & Musical Industries, Ltd.,* 155 F.Supp. 892 (S.D.N.Y. 1957) (foreign parent).

[10]See *In the Matter of Grand Jury Investigation of the Shipping Industry, supra; In the Matter of Grand Jury Subpoenas Duces Tecum,* 72 F. Supp. 1013 (S.D.N.Y. 1947).

[11]See *In re Investigation of World Arrangements with Relation to the Production, Transportation, Refining and Distribution of Petroleum, supra.*

[12]See, e.g., *Société International v. Rogers,* 357 U.S. 197 (1958).

[13]See, e.g., *Application of Chase Manhattan Bank,* 297 F.2d 611 (2d. Cir. 1962); *Ings v. Ferguson,* 282 F.2d 149 (2d. Cir. 1960).

[14]*Impact of Multinational Corporations on Development and on International Relations, supra,* p. 55.

[15]See *United States v. Marine Bancorporation, Inc.,* 418 U.S. 602 (1974); *United States v. General Dynamics Corp.,* 415 U.S. 486 (1974).

[16]See *United States v. National Association of Securities Dealers,* 95 S. Ct. 2427 (1975); *Gordon v. New York Stock Exchange Inc.,* 95 S. Ct. 1113 (1975).

An Overview of the Direction of U.S. Antitrust Law – Problems of the Multinational – 2

James A. Rahl *

WHAT SPECIAL ANTITRUST problems arise because a company is multi-national, transnational or international?

The U.N. Group of Eminent Persons, which reported last year, pointed in particular to the following: (1) allocation of selling markets among subsidiaries, thus hampering the ability of some of them to export and thereby damaging the host country's foreign trade; (2) using restrictive patent and know-how license practices to restrict exports, to prevent host country acquisition of the benefits of the technology, and to restrict sources of supply of goods needed to practice the technology licensed; (3) using prices for transfer of goods among the enter-prise's subsidiaries which are artificial as compared with open market prices, and which may sometimes discriminate against, and sometimes for, given sub-sidiaries, with alleged anticompetitive consequences; and (4) making acquisitions and entering into joint ventures which may unbalance and sometimes threaten the survival of host country industries and markets.[1]

In the United States, there has also been attention to the broader question of whether multinational firms enjoy some special advantage or immunity through the inability of national governments to regulate their activities on an interna-tional scale, and because of the lack of international law to deal with these questions. I will first discuss in general the extent to which American antitrust law may regulate international activities. Then, I will discuss some of the specific practices already mentioned.

Application of U.S. Law to Foreign Operations of Foreign and American-owned Enterprises

It goes without saying that when a multinational firm operates directly in the United States, it is as subject to U.S. laws as any American firm with respect to those activities. But American law may reach beyond the firm's direct operations in the United States. It may apply to foreign parent companies for actions of their U.S. corporate subsidiaries. And it may also reach activities of the foreign companies themselves in their home countries or, in some circumstances, in third countries. American-owned multinational enterprises, of course, also face U.S. antitrust controls as to some of their operations abroad.

The extraterritorial scope of the American law has long been a subject of controversy. In this respect, it has been joined by the law of the European

*Dean, School of Law, Northwestern University.

Economic Community, as interpreted by the *Dyestuffs* case,[2] and by the German law, as set forth in Section 98 (2) of the Act Against Restraints of Competition.

I will first state the theoretical scope of the American law and then illustrate its practical application.

U.S. law may apply to any company, whatever its ownership or nationality, if the activities of the company are of the type which violate substantive rules of the law, and if the activities are carried out in American interstate or foreign trade, or substantially affect such trade. This is what Congress has done in the Sherman Act, and the courts have repeatedly sustained it. It may be somewhat startling to realize that a recent study shows that up to May, 1973, the Department of Justice had filed almost 250 antitrust cases involving foreign trade in some way, and in not one did the government lose on the ground that the suit was beyond the international scope of the statute.[3] In many of these cases, there were foreign company defendants.

The broad extraterritorial application of the Sherman Act was underscored by the *Aluminum* case in 1945,[4] which held that the Act could be applied to a conspiracy composed entirely of foreign companies that agreed not to export to the United States, even though the conspiracy was formed and carried out in foreign countries. This principle has been endorsed by Section 18 of the American Law Institute's Restatement of Foreign Relations Law of the United States, and this gives it substantial standing in the American courts. Applicability of the Act is all the easier, of course, if one of the foreign companies is operating in the United States, or if one of the conspirators is a U.S. company. There have been many judgments against cartels of the latter kind, but there have been few like *Aluminum*, involving only foreign firms.

It is no defense that the activities of foreign firms are lawful under the law of their own or of third countries. The only recognized exception for foreign law is where the firm is *required* by foreign law to pursue the course of action which has resulted in the U.S. antitrust suit. For example, in the *Inter-American Refining Co.* case,[5] a lower U.S. court held it a valid defense against a boycott charge where the Venezuelan Government had ordered certain U.S. oil companies operating in Venezuela not to sell Venezuelan oil to a U.S. buyer engaged in selling the refined product outside the United States.

This defense of foreign government compulsion has been recognized by the Department of Justice, and I would consider it reliable as to activities in foreign markets, although it is not clear what kinds of compulsion will suffice; for example, if all that will happen is damage liability for breach of contract, the law is now clear. But suppose a foreign government were to order two multinational companies under its jurisdiction to agree upon selling prices in sales in the United States? Such a case has not been decided to my knowledge, but I doubt that American courts would permit U.S. law to be undermined in this way.

A further qualification may exist as to this defense of foreign government compulsion. Suppose a company operating in a foreign country *persuades* the foreign government to issue an order compelling firms to engage in conduct that restrains competition affecting American commerce? This persuasion might be through simple lobbying, or through agreement, or even possibly through "gifts" or bribery of which we have heard a good deal in the American newspapers lately. In *Occidental Petroleum*,[6] a lower U.S. court has held that persuasion of a foreign government by an American company operating abroad is not protected, although there are U.S. Supreme Court decisions holding that persuasion of *American* government officials by U.S. firms is immune.[7]

May *foreign* firms safely persuade the U.S. Government to order restrictive anticompetitive action? I should think that they would receive the benefit of the same rule applied to U.S. firms. May foreign firms persuade *foreign* governments to order restrictive action in the foreign firm's home country? in a third country? I simply cannot predict how this might be decided.

While foreign government compulsion, absent inducement of such complusion by the defendants, may be immune, interference by a foreign government with enforcement procedures by U.S. courts will sometimes be resisted. An American court has ordered persons under its jurisdiction to produce documents located in the Canadian Province of Quebec, for example, despite a Quebec statute prohibiting this.[8] And in the *Ampicillin* antitrust case, the U.S. court ordered a British parent company to answer interrogatories.[9] When the British Government ordered the company not to answer, the U.S. court stated that it would deprive the company of the right to advance defenses in the case: ultimately, the British order was modified and the U.S. court rescinded its penalizing order. Of course, the U.S. court had the upper hand in this case. If it did not, as in the old *duPont-ICI* case,[10] where a British court ordered a British company not to comply with an American antitrust court order to grant licenses of British patents, the U.S. court may give up in the name of "comity." "Comity" may sometimes be a euphemism for lack of practical power.

Of course, American law cannot be applied to any company unless what we call "personal jurisdiction" is obtained over that company through valid service of process. In general, there must be enough contact on the part of the company with the United States to satisfy constitutional requirements of "due process of law" in serving the company with process and ordering it to submit to the American court. An agent in the United States will generally be sufficient for this. Does the presence of a U.S. subsidiary of a foreign parent supply a basis for jurisdiction? In some cases, the courts have said that mere ownership is not enough, but that the parent may be found to control the subsidiary in such a way as to make it an agent or the alter ego of the parent.[11] In practice, unless the foreign parent gives the subsidiary almost full autonomy, it is likely to be subject to American antitrust court control.

A foreign company having no U.S. subsidiary and no agent in the United States may be immune from service of process unless it carries on business activities of some substantial kind in the United States. Selling and administering an insurance contract in an American state by mail has been held sufficient in an analogous case.[12] It is doubtful, however, that mere export sales to the United States alone would give jurisdiction. But further activities by an exporter in the United States concerning advertising, selling, servicing, collection of debts, etc., would probably give jurisdiction.

Actual service of process may be made in various ways, including sometimes by registered mail, or directly in the home country of the foreign firm if this is acceptable to the foreign government. Even in the absence of personal service, it may be possible for the government to seize goods of a foreign firm which is held to be violating the antitrust law, under a little-used section of the Sherman Act, but this is very rare.

There have been discussions lately about the possibility of an antitrust suit against the oil-producing nations' cartel for price fixing of oil exported to the United States. The biggest issue here might be that of sovereign immunity, and the principle that American antitrust law does not apply to government action. Such immunity is probably lost when the foreign government engages in direct business activity in the market. It seems to me, therefore, that such a suit could be filed, and that service of process would not be difficult. If the latter were a problem, there might still be an action to seize oil in transit or other assets. But this does not seem to me to be a very realistic idea from a political point of view, and I doubt that the U.S. Government will do it. It would still be open, however, to a private party, such as an American buyer of foreign oil, to file a private suit.

U.S. Government Enforcement Policy

In practice, the Department of Justice does not go to the limits of the theories discussed above. Partly because of many foreign complaints in the past over the extraterritorial application of American law, and lately because of concern that overzealous enforcement could hurt American business abroad, the Department of Justice has emphasized that it does not seek to push matters to possible extremes. Policy statements by high officials have repeatedly indicated that the antitrust laws will be used primarily in two classes of cases: (1) to prevent foreign firms from substantially lessening competition in the American domestic market, or in U.S. imports; and (2) to prevent arrangements that unduly restrict the opportunities of American firms to export to foreign markets.[13]

A high Department of Justice official, Donald Baker, stated that the government is not interested in application of the law to activities in foreign markets, either by foreign or by U.S. firms, where the above U.S. interests are not substantially affected.[14] For example, theoretically the law might be applied against price fixing, resale price maintenance, and other restrictions in foreign markets, if the agreements are made in the course of U.S. foreign commerce, or if movement of goods from the United States is affected by them. But the government says it will not sue unless adverse impact on U.S. interests is clear. Mr. Baker has also said that the Sherman Act should not be applied even to substantial restraints of competition in U.S. export commerce, or by U.S. firms in foreign countries, if the only victims of the restraints are foreigners. Export cartels operated by Americans thus would generally be all right even without the exemptions afforded to some by the Webb-Pomerene Act.[15] This view is not sustained by case law, however.

Application to Certain Transactions

Enough has been said to indicate that the multinational firm may become entangled in American antitrust law in various ways, and on the other hand that a great part of its life in foreign countries may be lived without fear of U.S. antitrust law. Let us consider the specific questions mentioned at the beginning.

Allocation of Markets

The first is that of allocation of markets by a multinational firm amongst different parts or subsidiaries of its enterprise. Assume that the firm arranges for its German subsidiary to sell in Europe but not in the United States, and vice versa for its American subsidiary. Variations of this example may be imagined. If these parts of the enterprise are not incorporated, American antitrust law generally will not apply at all to the agreements, instructions or arrangements within the enterprise.[16] If, however, separate corporations, i.e., legal persons, are involved, American law can be applied, and it may reach not only express agreements, but also implied agreements, or "practical" working arrangements among the different corporate units. It sometimes is said that all that is needed is to avoid making agreements in the intraenterprise setting. I believe that German officials at one stage took the position that if there were no agreements, but only operating instructions from parent to subsidiary, German antitrust under Section 1 of the German Act would not apply. One cannot avoid American antitrust law, however, merely by avoiding formal agreements and relying instead upon informal understandings.

Nevertheless, in the example I have put of intraenterprise territorial allocation, the Department of Justice would in all likelihood not file suit. It has made this clear a number of times, because it has endorsed the view of the Report of the Attorney General's National Committee to Study the Antitrust Laws in 1955 that the Sherman Act should not apply to intraenterprise agreements that merely regulate internally the prices, products and divisions of functions of various parts of the enterprise.[17] This comes close to what I understand to be the rule in the European Common Market under *Christiani & Nielsen* and other cases.[18]

If, however, the multinational has intraenterprise agreements that are intended to coerce, boycott or otherwise restrain the competition of outsiders to the enterprise, the U.S. Government may well proceed on an intraenterprise conspiracy theory. Moreover, private parties are not held back by government policies, and are free to claim damages resulting from, for example, a refusal to sell by a multinational's subsidiary pursuant to an intraenterprise division of markets agreement. A private suit against United Fruit Company for refusal to sell bananas to plaintiff in Honduras succeeded a number of years ago on an intraenterprise basis.[19] Agreements involving the operations of corporate joint ventures are on a different footing from agreements involving wholly owned subsidiaries, and should be analyzed in much the same way as agreements among independent companies.

Licensing

A second question is that of certain international aspects of licensing. Perhaps the biggest and most frequent complaint about licensing of patents and know-how is that such licensing may be used to restrict exports, either expressly or through licensing different licensees in different nations under only the patents

85

of their respective nations. This may produce the effect of export restriction and of territorial market division among the licensees.

American law has no counterpart of the developing Common Market rule that territory within the Common Market may not be divided by the patentee through the practice of relying upon national patent laws to bar cross-boundary sales in the Common Market of goods produced and sold under license of the patentee. Our Justice Department has stated that one may retain rights under American patents, and grant licenses under foreign patents to others, relying upon patent law, and possibly tariff or customs laws, to prevent cross-boundary sales.[20]

The Department, however, may attack *explicit* restrictive provisions in patent licenses which prohibit exports from, or imports to, the United States, although it is not concerned with restrictions on sales between foreign countries. But in *Dunlop Co. v. Kelsey-Hayes Co.*[21] in 1973, a U.S. Court of Appeals held that restrictions in foreign patent licenses against sales to the United States were allowable. A Justice Department official has criticized this decision,[22] and, personally, I would be reluctant to rely upon it. In 1972, however, a Justice Department memorandum given to Congress indicated that territorial restrictions in licenses of unpatented know-how, preventing export from a foreign country to the United States might be allowable if reasonably necessary to protect the licenser in its retained business, and if not unduly restrictive.[23] There are problems of theory and analysis with this approach, and it has not received much support in the courts.

Transfer Pricing

A third question is that of transfer pricing among different parts of the multinational enterprise. The principal complaints noted in the report of the U.N. Group of Eminent Persons center around the claim that transfer prices do not always accord with market realities and may be artificially high or low. If "too high" to a subsidiary in a given third country, that subsidiary may be disabled from exporting because of higher costs. If "too low" in some situations, the beneficiary may have a cost advantage amounting to a kind of subsidy which enables it to undersell local competitors in the third country.

As far as American law is concerned, the only antitrust statute likely to be in point is the Robinson-Patman Act. This Act, with minor exceptions not pertinent here, applies only in cases of *discrimination* in price or services or facilities as between different buyers. It appears that the Act may be applied to sales by a parent company to a subsidiary,[24] and thus may apply to transfer prices between different corporate entities in a multinational enterprise. On the other hand, transfers between branches or divisions of the same corporation probably will not be considered to be transactions covered by the Act. Sales of goods of like grade and quality to different buyers at different prices are required for the Act to apply. Consequently, mere sales at a level considered "high" or "low" will not invoke the Act, if all sales are at the same price.

If a multinational enterprise sells to independent buyers at one price and sells or "transfers" the same kinds of goods to subsidiaries or related companies at a lower price, it may have trouble under the Act. An important qualification is that the Act applies only to goods sold for "use, consumption or resale" within the United States or other territory under its jurisdiction. The exact meaning of this provision is unclear and it is subject to different interpretations. It is certain that the Act will apply, however, to a foreign company exporting to the United States and charging different prices in those sales. It is also possible, but not certain, that the Act could apply if prices charged in sales to U.S. buyers differ from prices charged to buyers in other countries.

If the transaction does fall within the Act, then of course the question remains whether the substantive provisions have been violated.

[1] United Nations Department of Economic and Social Affairs, *The Impact of Multinational Corporations on Development and on International Relations,* Report of Group of Eminent Persons, 83-86 U.N. Doc. E/5500/ Rev. 1 ST/ESA/6 (1974).

[2] *Imperial Chemical Industries, Ltd. v. Commission of the European Communities,* [1971-1973 Transfer Binder] CCH Comm. Mkt. Rep. ¶ 8161 (E.C. Ct. of Justice 1972).

[3] W. Fugate, *Foreign Commerce and the Antitrust Laws* App. B, at 498 (2d ed. 1973).

[4] *United States v. Aluminum Co. of America,* 148 F.2d 416 (2d Cir. 1945).

[5] *Interamerican Refining Corp. v. Texaco Maracaibo, Inc.,* 307 F. Supp. 1291 (D. Del. 1970).

[6] *Occidental Petroleum Corp. v. Buttes Gas & Oil Co.,* 331 F. Supp. 92 (C.D. Cal. 1971), *aff'd per curiam,* 461 F.2d 1261 (9th Cir. 1972), *cert. denied,* 409 U.S. 950 (1972).

[7] *Eastern Railroad Presidents Conf. v. Noerr Motor Freight, Inc.,* 365 U.S. 127 (1961); *United Mine Workers of America v. Pennington,* 381 U.S. 657 (1965); *cf. California Motor Transport Co. v. Trucking Unlimited,* 404 U.S. 508 (1972).

[8] *American Industrial Contracting, Inc. v. Johns-Manville Corp.,* 326 F. Supp. 879 (W.D. Pa. 1971).

[9] *In Re Ampicillin Antitrust Litigation,* Civil No. 822-70 (D.D.C., filed Mar. 19, 1970).

[10] *British Nylon Spinners, Ltd. v. Imperial Chem. Indus., Ltd.,* [1953] Ch. 19, [1952] 2 All E. R. 780 (C.A.) (injunction by lower court against compliance with U.S. decree affirmed; American Decree was "intrusion" on British sovereignty); *British Nylon Spinners, Ltd. v. Imperial Chem. Indus., Ltd.,* [1955] Ch. 37, [1954] 3 All E.R. 88 (Ch.) (declaratory judgment granting specific performance of the ICI-BNS license.).

[11] *Dobson v. Farbenfabriken of Elderfeld Co.,* 206 Fed. 125 (E.D. Pa. 1913); *United States v. United States Alkali Export Assn.,* 1946-1947 *Trade Cas.* ¶ 57,481 (S.D.N.Y. 1946); *United States v. Imperial Chemical Industries, Ltd.,* 100 F. Supp. 504 (S.D.N.Y. 1951); *Dobbins v. Kawasaki Motors Corp.,* 362 F. Supp. 54 (D. Ore. 1974).

[12] *McGee v. International Life Ins. Co.,* 355 U.S. 220 (1957).

[13] Address by Donald I. Baker, Director of Policy Planning, Antitrust Division, before the New York State Bar Ass'n., New York City, Jan. 24, 1973, reprinted in 5 CCH Trade Reg. Rep. ¶ 50,161, at 55,283 (1974); Address by Keith I. Clearwaters, Special Asst. to the Asst. Attorney General, Antitrust Division, before the Ass'n. of General Counsel, Hot Springs, Virginia, May 4, 1973, reprinted in 5 CCH Trade Reg. Rep. ¶ 50,169, at 55,300 (1974).

[14] D. Baker, Antitrust and World Trade: Tempest in an International Teapot?, 8 *Cornell Int'l L.J.* 16,31 (1974).

[15] *Id., at 28; cf.* J.A. Rahl, American Antitrust and Foreign Operations: What Is Covered?, 8 *Cornell Int'l L.J.* 1,8 (1974); J.A. Rahl, A Rejoinder, 8 *Cornell Int'l L.J.* 42,43-44 (1974).

[16] *Nelson Radio & Supply Co., Inc. v. Motorola, Inc.*, 200 F.2d 911 (5th Cir. 1952), *cert. denied*, 345 U.S. 925 (1953); *Joseph E. Seagram & Sons, Inc. v. Hawaiian Oke & Liquors, Ltd.*, 416 F.2d 71 (9th Cir. 1969), *cert. denied*, 396 U.S. 1062 (1970), *reh. denied*, 397 U.S. 1003 (1970).

[17] Letter from Asst. Attorney General Richard W. McLaren to Thomas J. O'Connell, General Counsel, Board of Governors of the Federal Reserve System, Feb. 22, 1971, printed in BNA *Antitrust & Trade Regulation Report*, D-1, D-4 (1971).

[18] *Christiani and Neilsen N.V.*, [1965-1969 Transfer Binder] CCH Comm. Mkt. Rep. ¶ 9308 (E.C. 1969).

[19] *Sanib Corp. v. United Fruit Co.*, 135 F. Supp. 764 (S.D.N.Y. 1955).

[20] Memorandum of the Department of Justice Concerning Antitrust and Foreign Commerce, reprinted in 5 CCH Trade Reg. Rep. ¶ 50,129 at 55,210 (1975).

[21] 484 F.2d 407 (6th Cir. 1973), *cert. denied*, 415 U.S. 917 (1973).

[22] J. Davidow, "United States Antitrust Laws and International Transfers of Technology — The Government View," B.E. Hawk, ed., in *Annual Proceedings of the Fordham Corporate Law Institute* 177 (1974).

[23] Memorandum, *supra* note 20, at 55,209.

[24] *Danko v. Shell Oil Co.*, 115 F. Supp. 886 (E.D.N.Y. 1953); *Mississippi Petroleum, Inc. v. Vermont Gas Sys., Inc.*, 1972 *Trade Cas.* ¶ 73,843 (S.D. Miss. 1972); *cf. Reines Distribs., Inc. v. Admiral Corp.*, 256 F. Supp. 581 (S.D.N.Y. 1966).

New Departures in Trade Regulation Enforcement

Miles W. Kirkpatrick *

QUESTIONS CONCERNING new departures in trade regulation enforcement are both timely and important. The year 1975 saw major legislation go into effect, and even more far-reaching changes are being proposed.

Why have so many changes been suggested recently? A major reason is that there have been new pressures on trade regulation policy. The rise of an organized consumer movement, a phenomenon which has made its appearance in almost all industrial nations, has been a major factor in contributing to both the number and the type of demands made upon the government in the area of trade regulation. Such demands are difficult for the government to ignore, because they are presented by a wide range of consumer organizations on behalf of an increasingly aware citizenry.

A second source of pressure on trade regulation policy has been the recent world economic conditions, experienced in the United States as a combination of inflation and stagnation. Such conditions have raised public concern about the possible relation between industrial concentration and prices. This concern was reflected in remarks at the White House Conference on Inflation in 1974, following which President Ford expressed the view to a joint session of Congress that: "To increase productivity and contain prices, we must end restrictive and costly practices whether instituted by government, industry, labor or others." The President proposed to attain this end in part through a "return to the vigorous enforcement of antitrust law."[1]

What response is likely to these new pressures on, and increased public and governmental concern with, trade regulation policy? The exact restrictions imposed by the antitrust laws are not clear. The broad prohibitions of the Sherman Act, the Clayton Act, or the Federal Trade Commission Act, are written more like constitutional provisions, allowing great leeway for executive and judicial interpretation.[2] While precise prohibitions are thus unclear, the general thrust is clear: Competition is the value to be served. Indeed, the term "competition policy" may perhaps be much more descriptive of the aims than the term "antitrust policy." Recognition of competition as the paramount value of the United States trade regulation laws, does not, however, illuminate the best course to take to arrive at this ideal economic system.

In theory, there are two possible responses that could be made: (1) a substantive approach, *i.e.*, changes in the substantive provisions of the antitrust laws; or (2) a procedural approach, *i.e.*, changes in enforcement mechanisms

*Partner in law firm of Morgan, Lewis & Bockius, Washington, D.C.

without altering existing substantive provisions. While a substantive approach might seem the more fundamental, and thus more likely to be pursued, I believe that there will be very little change in this direction in the foreseeable future.

One reason is that there is considerable controversy in this area between two schools of economic thought: the structuralist school and the behavioralist school.[3] The structuralists contend that the market structure in which a firm operates is the critical determinant of that firm's pricing, output, innovation and investment decisions. These economists hold that an industry's structure determines the industry's economic performance, as well as its economic conduct. More specifically, this economic theory suggests that an industry characterized by certain structural features – particularly high concentration, a high degree of product differentiation, advertising and high barriers to entry – will also be characterized by higher-than-competitive profits and price levels.[4] While many researchers have found such a statistical relationship between market structure and performance, the issue is not yet resolved to the satisfaction of the economic community as a whole.[5]

The behavioralist school, by contrast, de-emphasizes the effect of the size of the firms in an industry, their number, and their distribution. Rather, these economists emphasize a firm's conduct, not its size. They argue that each firm and industry must be judged on its own merits, and they dismiss a litmus test of market share, either individually or collectively, as a critical determinant of ability to control price or exclude competition. They suggest that policing the behavior of firms through a vigilant program of enforcement by the government, coupled with the threat of private treble-damage actions by those directly injured by infractions, provides the best assurance of the benefits of competition.[6]

These theoretical differences, and the lack of sufficient empirical evidence with which to confirm the overall validity of the structural approach, means that there is unlikely to be any widespread agreement on the type of substantive changes which would be appropriate in the trade regulation laws. This lack of agreement over substantive theory may be seen in the continuing controversy not only over various legislative proposals but also over three major structural suits: the action by the Department of Justice against AT&T, calling for divestiture of its manufacturing division;[7] the actions by the Federal Trade Commission against the nation's four major cereal companies;[8] and the eight largest petroleum companies.[9]

A similar controversy rages over the proposed Industrial Reorganization Act, introduced by Senator Philip A. Hart several years ago, and reintroduced in 1975 as S. 1959. This proposal, often referred to as the Hart economic deconcentration bill, is designed to break up into smaller units many large corporations in concentrated markets. Among other things, the bill would declare it presumptively unlawful for any four or fewer firms to have accounted for 50 percent or more of relevant market sales in three years preceding the filing of a complaint. The only defenses to court-ordered divestiture under such circumstances would be to show either that the defendant's market power had been achieved solely through the ownership of valid patents, lawfully acquired and used, or that divestiture would result in a loss of substantial economies of scale. Further, an Industrial Reorganization Commission, which would be established to prosecute violations of the proposed bill, would study and develop plans of reorganization of seven broadly defined industries, regardless of whether any corporation in those industries was found to be in violation of the Act.

The proposal has been severely criticized, and it has been reported that even Senator Hart and his staff candidly admit that the bill faces a near-insurmountable uphill struggle before it becomes law.[10] Such a reaction illustrates the difficulty facing any proposal for major substantive changes in the trade regulation laws.

A similar uncertainty over the most desirable substantive approach is illustrated by the shift in the Supreme Court's interpretation of Section 7 of the Clayton Act, the last major piece of substantive trade regulation legislation. In *United States v. General Dynamics Corp.,* the Court upheld a horizontal merger of two coal producers, each of which enjoyed a substantial share of a concentrated market.[11] The government proved that a small number of leading producers dominated the coal producing industry; that there had been a trend toward increasing concentration; and that the merger significantly enhanced the acquiring company's market share.[12]

While the Court acknowledged that, under prior horizontal decisions, this statistical showing was sufficient to make out a *prima facie* case of illegality, the Court reached back to its decision in *Brown Shoe Co. v. United States,* decided twelve years earlier, for the proposition that while market-share percentages are "the primary index of market power. . .only a further examination of the particular market — its structure, history and probable future — can provide the appropriate setting for judging the probable anticompetitive effect of the merger."[13]

Although it remains to be seen whether the Supreme Court will now permit the defendant in a horizontal merger case to show that the relevant market, though concentrated, behaves not anticompetitively as economic theory would have it, but in a highly competitive fashion, Justice Powell's opinion for the majority in *United States v. Marine Bancorporation, Inc.,* the other Section 7 defeat visited on the government in 1974, indicates that the defendants may offer such proof in a potential competition case where the defendants may offer such proof in a potential competition case where the existence of a concentrated market is an essential element of the theory of violation.[14] *Marine Bancorporation* "graphically illustrates the present Supreme Court's unwillingness to accept, without evidentiary support, economic theory and mere possibilities of competitive impact as dispositive of a Section 7 case."[15] Although the market concentration ratios in that case were high, justifying a presumption that the market was not vigorously competitive, the Court made it clear that the defendant banks were nevertheless entitled to attempt to prove that "the concentration ratios. . .did not accurately depict the [market's] economic characteristics. . . ." In this connection, Justice Powell cited *General Dynamics* for the proposition that statistics "can be unreliable indicators of actual market behavior."

While it would be possible to argue that these two cases are limited to their unique factual contexts, they appear to be highly significant indicators of what has been called the "new antitrust majority's"[16] changed outlook on Section 7 of the Clayton Act.[17] But more broadly, these decisions illustrate the uncertainty of the Supreme Court regarding the substantive content of a major trade regulation statute.

I think it is clear, then, that because of this uncertainty over the most desirable substantive approach, coupled with the increased, and now organized, pressures for change in trade regulation policy, the foreseeable future should show increased attention to improvements in the *procedures* for the enforcement of trade regulation policy. It has been the view of some of those in the government, who are charged with the enforcement of the antitrust laws, that the substantive statutes now on the books are quite adequate for the task. The Chief of the Antitrust Division of the Department of Justice recently commented that, "our problems have been more procedural and lack of resources than problems of substantive authority."[18]

This current concentration upon improvements in procedures for trade regulation enforcement is evident in developments concerning all of the institutions concerned with trade regulation policy. There has been major recent activity in Congress, both with respect to enacted legislation and to proposed bills. While many of these new laws and proposed amendments have been subjected to severe, and often justified, criticism, it is clear that they will substantially affect both the possibility of an action being brought for violations of the trade regulation laws, and the severity of the penalty that will be imposed if a violation is found.

As a result of the recent enactment of the Antitrust Procedures and Penalties Act, the stakes are now much higher for businesses undertaking activities that run the risk of violating the federal antitrust laws.[19] Among other things, this measure increases the fines for Sherman Act violations from $50,000 to $1 million for corporations, and from $50,000 to $100,000 for individuals. It also makes the commission of a Sherman Act offense a felony, and increases the maximum prison sentence from one to three years.[20] While it is still very unclear how great the actual deterrent value of such possible criminal penalties will be, it is more than clear that the potential risk for businessmen has been vastly increased.

Another major feature of the new Antitrust Procedures and Penalties Act radically changes the procedures that govern consent judgments in government antitrust suits. Amending Section 5 of the Clayton Act, the new law requires that, before a consent decree is approved, the Justice Department must file a "competitive impact statement" that explains the proposal and its anticipated effect on competition, and gives a description and evaluation of the alternatives considered by the government.[21] Upon receiving any comments concerning the proposed consent decree, the district court must then determine that the proposed judgment operates in the "public interest."[22]

In announcing the signing of the new Act, President Ford noted that he had called for further antitrust legislation, and reiterated his hope that the new Congress would carry that call forward. But it is not only Congress that has been involved in proposals for procedural reform in the trade regulation area.

The Ford Administration has been very concerned, not only with stimulating congressional activity, but also with regulatory reform aimed at reducing government regulation of business. President Ford's proposal for a National Commission on Regulatory Reform, which would examine individual regulatory schemes in major industries and develop recommendations for reduced government regulation of business, has been widely supported, even by many of those who head the independent agencies presently under attack.[23] As of late 1975, the President had sent two proposals to Congress: one to substantially curtail federal regulation of the domestic airline industry and the other to sharply reduce federal regulation of the railroad industry.[24]

While serious inefficiencies have resulted from overregulation of business by government, any reform commission should be empowered to look at the operations and programs of *all* government agencies and offices.[25] As I have previously observed, "the policy and programs of the Executive branch are capable of an equal amount of competitive misdirection, (and) have as far-reaching economic and competitive effects as those of the regulatory agencies."[26]

In addition to his proposals on deregulation, President Ford has stated that his Administration will propose changes in other laws that restrain competition and deny buyers substantial savings. The President singled out the Robinson-Patman anti-price discrimination act, as a leading example of such a law.[27] He stated that the Act "discourages both large and small firms from cutting prices, and it also makes it harder for them to expand into new markets and to pass on to customers the cost-savings on large orders."[28]

I do not wish to enter into a discussion of the desirability of these recommendations. I mention them only to point out that they are not proposals for new substantive regulations. While the United States is hardly poised for a complete return to laissez-faire, I think it is clear that the current proposals from both the Congress and from the Administration are in the direction of less regulation in areas where regulation itself has become part of the problem, or of procedural innovations and improvements to use already existing substantive laws more effectively.

A similar trend is apparent in developments concerning the other major trade regulation enforcement arm of the government, the Federal Trade Commission. On January 4, 1975, President Ford signed into law the Magnuson-Moss Warranty Federal Trade Commission Improvement Act.[29] That legislation not only expands the jurisdictional reach of the Commission but also significantly bolsters its enforcement authority and clearly constitutes the most significant amendment to the FTC Act since its enactment in 1914.

The Act increases the Commission's power in five discrete areas: jurisdiction, rulemaking, civil penalties, consumer redress, and investigative authority. None of these provisions affect the substantive mandate of the Commission, but all greatly increase the Commission's ability to enforce that mandate.

For example, the expansion of FTC jurisdiction to include those practices "in or affecting" interstate commerce represents the broadest possible grant of jurisdiction to the Commission, removing any practical jurisdictional bars to the Commission's regulatory authority. Similarly, while the Commission was previously authorized to obtain reports and documentary evidence only from "corporations," the new statute broadens the Commission's investigative authority to cover persons and partnerships, in addition to corporations. The Act also authorizes the Commission to promulgate binding trade regulation rules proscribing unfair or deceptive acts or practices on an industrywide basis. While this grant of power is accompanied by various procedural safeguards, it is clear that this new enforcement authority will become a significant weapon in the Commission's arsenal.

The FTC Improvement Act not only increases the maximum recoverable civil penalty to $10,000 per each violation of a Commission rule or cease and desist order, but it also expands the circumstances under which the FTC can seek civil penalties.[30] Section 205 of the new Act permits the Commission to seek civil penalties, regardless of whether the Commission has entered a cease and desist order or whether there has been a violation of an industrywide trade regulation rule, so long as the Commission can prove that the company knowingly engaged in conduct that had been previously proscribed in a Commission proceeding. The possible far-reaching effect of this enforcement provision can be illustrated by the following example: The FTC enters an order against Company A, which becomes final. The Commission then mails a copy of the order to Company B, which is totally uninvolved in the prior proceeding. If Company B should subsequently violate the terms of that order, the FTC could bring suit, without any further administrative proceedings, for civil penalties in a federal district court against Company B. In effect, the entry of an order by the FTC against one company becomes a rule as to any company that has actual knowledge of the order.

The new Act also authorizes the FTC to institute civil actions to redress consumer injuries resulting from violations of Commission rules concerning unfair or deceptive practices or from violations of cease and desist orders issued by the Commission.[31] Such consumer redress can take the form of damages or restitution, and can also include rescission of contracts, public notification, and the like.

The consumer redress provision represents a highly significant extension of the Commission's remedial powers. It vastly increases the potential consequences of violations of the laws enforced by the Federal Trade Commission. In this, it is like so many of the enactments and proposed enactments I have discussed earlier. Business enterprises, for the first time, are now liable for consumer redress orders in the millions of dollars for violations of the FTC Act.[32]

As you might expect, there are a host of unresolved issues concerning the nature and scope of the FTC's new enforcement powers. There should be no uncertainty, however, as to the fact that these powers, coupled with the power granted to the Commission in late 1973 to seek preliminary injunctive relief, are important extensions of the FTC enforcement authority.[33] The Commission may seek such relief whenever it has reason to believe that a violation of the Act is occurring or about to occur, and that such relief would be in the public interest. I have previously referred to the FTC Improvement Act as "the legal equivalent of dynamite."[34] If so, it is an explosive which all businesses must in the future handle with care.

Finally, I would like to mention another procedural innovation, by another institution intimately concerned with trade regulation enforcement, the Judiciary. A novel procedural approach has recently been pursued by a federal district judge in California, who meted out an unusual sentence to eight corporate officers who pleaded "no contest" to government charges that they conspired to fix the prices of paper labels used on food, beverages and cosmetics.[35] The judge sentenced each of the corporate officers to three or six months' imprisonment, suspended the sentence, and gave a year's probation conditioned upon the defendants making twelve speeches on price fixing during the next year to business and civic groups. The defendants were also required to submit a written report to the court giving details of each such appearance and presentation, the composition of the group spoken to, and the response to the speech. The judge apparently devised the speech-making provision while casting about for a nonprison sentencing alternative — which would still carry a deterrent effect — in an effort to emphasize that trade regulation problems often arise as a result of a lack of education on the part of all concerned.[36] Whatever the final judgment on the utility or desirability of this procedure, it again points out the widespread concern over effective enforcement among all institutions in the trade regulation area.

It may be useful to conclude by asking about the implications of these enforcement innovations in trade regulation policy. As to the enforcement agencies themselves, the shift almost certainly means increased activity, but with no greater theoretical coherence or consistent purpose than exists at present. The new procedural tools should, however, at the least, vastly improve the efficiency of the enforcement activities undertaken. As to the parties who will be affected by this increased activity, the private businessmen, there is clearly the increased possibility of actions for violations of the trade regulation laws, with much more stringent penalties should a violation be established.

All of this points to the imperative necessity for close attention to the competitive effects of business decisions, and the thoughtful preparation of internal antitrust and trade regulation compliance programs. The procedural innovations, which I have outlined, must be matched by *preventive* innovations on the part of the businesses affected if trade regulation enforcement is to assist — and not hinder — the competitive process.

[1] *New York Times,* October 9, 1974.

[2] 15 U.S.C. §§1-7 (1970); 15 U.S.C. §§12-27, 44 (1970); and 15 U.S.C. §§41-51 (1970), respectively.

[3] See Irwin & Barrett, "Antitrust Enforcement in the United States: Market Structure versus Market Conduct," 1974 *Wash. U.L.O.* 37, 38-42.

[4] For this view, see C. Kaysen & D. Turner, *Antitrust Policy: An Economic and Legal Analysis* (1959); J. Bain, *Industrial Organization* (2d ed. 1968); W. Mueller, *A Primer on Monopoly and Competition* (1970); F. Scherer, *Industrial Market Structure and Economic Performance* (1970); W. Shepard, *Market Power and Economic Welfare* (1970); J. Blair, *Economic Concentration: Structure, Behavior and Public Policy* (1972); Irwin & Barrett, *supra* Note 3.

[5] See generally B. Bock, *Concentration, Oligopoly, and Profit: Concepts vs. Data* (1972); Demsetz, "Two Systems of Belief about Monopoly," *Industrial Concentration: The New Learning*, 164-83 (H. Goldschmid, H. Mann, & J. Weston, eds., 1974); Posner "Antitrust Policy and the Supreme Court: An Analysis of the Restricted Distribution, Horizontal Merger and Potential Competition Decisions," 75 *Colum. L. Rev.* 282, 312-13 (1975); Dalton & Penn, "Antitrust and the Snare of Published Profit Data: The Need for 'Line-of-Business' Reporting," 7 *Antitrust L. & Econ. Rev.* 75 (1974); Adams, "Market Structure and Corporate Power: The Horizontal Dominance Hypothesis Reconsidered," 74 *Colum. L. Rev.* 1276 (1974); Rhoades, "Concentration – Profitability Relationship: Policy Implications and Some Empirical Evidence," 18 *Antitrust Bulletin* 333 (1973).

[6] For this view, see Handler, "Antitrust – Myth and Reality in an Inflationary Era," 50 *N.Y.U.L. Rev.* 211 (1975); Brozen, "Concentration and Profits: Does Concentration Matter?," 19 *Antitrust Bulletin*, 381 (1974).

[7] *United States v. American Tel. & Tel. Co.*, No. 74-1698, 5 *Trade Reg. Rep.*, ¶45,074, at p. 53,589; see *Antitrust in a Rapidly Changing Economy*, The Conference Board, 1975, pp. 37-38.

[8] *Kellogg Co.*, No. 8883 [1970-1973 FTC Complaints & Orders Transfer Binder] *Trade Reg. Rep.* ¶19,898, at p. 21,915 (FTC, announced April 26, 1972). See Mueller, "Advertising, Monopoly, and the FTC's Breakfast Cereal Case: An 'Attack on Advertising,' " 6 *Antitrust L. & Econ. Rev.* 59 (1973).

[9] *Exxon Corp.*, No. 8934, 3 *Trade Reg. Rep.* ¶20,388, at p. 20,269 (FTC, announced July 17, 1973).

[10] See, *e.g.*, Handler, *supra* note 6, at 256-61. BNA *Antitrust & Trade Reg. Report* No. 717, at A-11 (1975). See Hart, "Restucturing the Oligopoly Sector: The Case for a New 'Industrial Reorganization' Act," 5 *Antitrust L. & Econ. Rev. 35 (1972);* "Note,The Industrial Reorganization Act: An Antitrust Proposal to Restructure the American Economy," 73 *Colum. L. Rev.* 635 (1973); "Note, Legislative Approach to Market Concentration: The Industrial Reorganization Act," 24 *Syr. L. Rev.* 1100 (1973).

[11] 415 U.S. 486 (1974).

[12] Id. at 494-96.

[13] 370 U.S. 294 (1962); Id. at 322 n.38, *quoted in* 415 U.S. at 498.

[14] 418 U.S. 602 (1974).

[15] Robinson, "Recent Antitrust Developments: 1974," 75 *Colum L. Rev.* 243,254 (1975).

[16] 418 U.S. at 631, 642.

[17] There has been extensive discussion of these cases, and their import. See, *e.g.*, Robinson, *supra* note 15, at 143-60; Posner, *supra* note 5, at 310-13; Fox, "Antitrust, Mergers, and the Supreme Court: The Politics of Section 7 of the Clayton Act," 26 *Mercer L. Rev.* 389 (1975); Horsley, *Marine Bancorporation, Connecticut National Bank* [418 U.S. 656 (1974)] and "Potential Competition: A Critique," 55 *B.U.L. Rev.* 3 (1975); Moyer, *"United States v. General Dynamics Corporation:* An Interpretation," 20 *Antitrust Bulletin* 1 (1975); Comment, "The Potential Competition Doctrine after *Marine Bancorporation,"* 63 *Geo. L.J.* 969 (1975).

[18] BNA *Antitrust & Trade Reg. Report* No. 714, at A-22 (1975). There are those who disagree with the necessity for any procedural reforms. See the view of Professor Handler, in Handler, *supra* note 6 at 265.

[19] Pub. L. No. 93-528, 88 Stat. 1706 (1974), codified in sections of 15, 47, 49 U.S.C.A. (Supp. 1975).

[20] 15 U.S.C.A. §§1-3 (Supp. 1975).

[21] The "competitive impact statement" must be published in the Federal Register for at least 60 days prior to the entry of the decree. The law also requires that a summary of the impact statement and of the proposed decree be published in newspapers of general circulation for two weeks, beginning at least 60 days prior to the decree's entry. During

this period, the Justice Department is obligated to "receive and consider" any written complaints relating to the proposed decree. For a criticism of the new Act, see Handler, *supra* note 6 at 227-44.

[22] It is possible that far-reaching changes in the quality of antitrust and trade regulation opinions may result from one of the more technical changes in the new Act. By virtue of amendments to the Expediting Act of 1903 (15 U.S.C.A. §28 [Supp. 1975]), rather than proceeding directly to the U.S. Supreme Court, appeals in antitrust injunction actions now generally lie with the U.S. Courts of Appeal. As Professor Posner has recently noted, "since most of the important antitrust cases have been Justice Department equity cases, the Expediting Act has eliminated what would otherwise have been a substantial body of non-Supreme Court appellate decisions in the antitrust field and has reduced the number of circuit judges who are experienced in antitrust matters (which has had bad effects on the private and FTC cases that come before the circuit courts). The Court has, in short, had less help from the circuit judges in the antitrust field than in others." Posner, *supra* note 5, at 327. It is possible that, over the long term, the quality of opinions in the trade regulation area may improve as a result of this increased deliberation.

[23] See BNA *Antitrust & Trade Reg. Report* No. 690, at A-17 to A-22 (1974). See Hearings on Regulatory Reform before the Senate Committee on Government Operations, 93d Cong., 2d Sess., pts. 1-2 (1974). The bill drafted by the Administration (S. 4145; H.R. 17417) would set up a special commission to devote one year and $500,000 to the drafting of reform recommendations for the independent regulatory agencies.

[24] *Congressional Quarterly*, October 11, 1975, at 2176 (the proposal is entitled the Aviation Act of 1975) and *Congressional Quarterly*, May 24, 1975, at 1100 (the proposal is entitled the Railroad Revitalization Act of 1975).

[25] See generally *Promoting Competition in Regulated Markets* (A. Phillips, ed. 1975).

[26] BNA *Antitrust & Trade Reg. Report* No. 690, at A-18 (1974).

[27] 15 U.S.C. §13 (1970). An exhaustive recent reassessment may be found in Elias, "Robinson-Patman: Time for Rechiseling," 26 *Mercer L. Rev.* 689 (1975).

[28] The President's Remarks to the 63rd Annual Meeting of the Chamber of Commerce of the United States, April 28, 1975.

[29] P.L. No. 93-637, 88 Stat. 2183 (1974), codified in sections of 15 U.S.C., amending sections of the Federal Trade Commission Act, 15 U.S.C. §§41-58 (1970).

[30] 15 U.S.C.A. §45(a)(1) (Supp. 1975); §46(a) (Supp. 1975); §57a(a)(1) (Supp. 1975); §45(m)(1)(A-B) (Supp. 1975).

[31] 15 U.S.C.A. §57b(a) (Supp. 1975).

[32] For a discussion of this aspect of the new Act, see "Note, *Heater v. FTC,* and the Federal Trade Commission Improvement Act: The FTC's Power to Order Restitution," 1975 *Duke L.J.* 379.

[33] 15 U.S.C.A. §53(b) (Supp. 1974).

[34] BNA *Antitrust & Trade Reg. Report* No. 698, at A-20 (1975).

[35] *United States v. H.S. Crocker Co., Inc.,* 5 Trade Reg. Rep. ¶45,074, at p. 53,563-3 (N.D. Cal. 1975).

[36] BNA *Antitrust & Trade Reg. Report* No. 689, at AA-1 (1974); No. 706, at AA-1 (1975).

Summary of Important U.S. Antitrust, Trade Regulation, and Antidumping Statutes

SHERMAN ANTITRUST ACT
(Enacted in 1890)

Section 1. Contacts, Combinations and Conspiracies in Restraint of Trade. Declares illegal "every contract, combination in the form of trust or otherwise, or conspiracy, in restraint of trade or commerce among the several States, or with foreign nations."* Provides that a violation of this section shall constitute a felony punishable, in the case of a corporation, by a fine of up to one million dollars, or, in the case of any other person, by a fine of up to one hundred thousand dollars and/or imprisonment for up to three years. [15 U.S.C. §1]

Section 2. Monopolizing, Attempts to Monopolize, Conspiracies to Monopolize Commerce. Declares that "every person who shall monopolize, or attempt to monopolize, or combine or conspire with any other person or persons, to monopolize any part of the trade or commerce among the several States, or with foreign nations, shall be deemed guilty of a felony." Punishment is the same as for violations of Section 1. [15 U.S.C. §2]

CLAYTON ACT
(Enacted in 1914)

Section 3. Exclusive Dealing and Tying Arrangements. Prohibits "any person engaged in commerce, in the course of such commerce, to lease or make a sale or contract for sale of . . . commodities, whether patented or unpatented, for use, consumption, or resale within the United States, [its territories or possessions], or fix a price . . . , or discount . . . , or rebate . . . [for such commodities], on the condition, agreement, or understanding that the lessee or purchaser thereof shall not use or deal in the . . . commodities of a competitor or competitors of the lessor or seller, where the effect . . . may be to substantially lessen competition or tend to create a monopoly in any line of commerce." [15 U.S.C. §14]

Section 7. Acquisitions of Stock or Assets of Corporations. Provides that "no corporation engaged in commerce shall acquire, directly or indirectly, the whole or any part of the stock or other share capital and no corporation subject to the jurisidiction of the Federal Trade Commission shall acquire the whole or any part of the assets of another corporation engaged also in commerce, where in any line of commerce in any section of the country, the effect of such acquisition may be substantially to lessen competition, or to tend to create a monopoly." [15 U.S.C. §18]

Section 8. Interlocking Directorates. Provides that "no person at the same time shall be a director in any two or more corporations, any one of which has capital, surplus, and undivided profits aggregating more than one million dollars, engaged in whole or in part in commerce, other than banks, banking associations, trust companies, and common carriers subject to the Act to regulate commerce, . . . , if such corporations are or shall have been theretofore, by virtue of their business and location of operation, competitors, so that the elimination of competition by agreement between them would constitute a violation of any of the provisions of any of the antitrust laws." [15 U.S.C. §19]

ROBINSON-PATMAN ACT
(Enacted in 1936 as an amendment
to the Clayton Act)

Section 2(a). Price Discrimination. Prohibits "any person engaged in commerce, in the course of such commerce, either directly or indirectly, to discriminate in price between different purchasers of commodities of like grade and quality, where either or any of the purchases involved in such discrimination are in commerce, where such commodities are sold for use, consumption, or resale within the United States, [its territories or possessions], and where the effect of such discrimination may be substantially to lessen competition or tend to create a monopoly in any line of commerce, or to injure, destroy, or prevent competition with any person who either grants or knowingly receives the benefit of such discrimination, or with customers of either of them." [15 U.S.C. §13(a)]

Section 2(a) is qualified by provisos (1) permitting price differentials which make only "due allowance for differences in the cost of manufacture, sale, or delivery resulting from the differing methods or quantities in which such commodities are . . . sold or delivered"; (2) authorizing the Federal Trade Commission to "establish quantity limits . . . as to particular commodities or classes of commodities, where it finds that available purchasers in greater quantities are so few as to render differentials on account thereof unjustly discriminatory or promotive of monopoly in any line of commerce"; and (3) permitting price changes "in response to changing conditions affecting the market for or the marketability of the goods concerned."

Section 2(b). Meeting Competition. Provides that a *prima facie* case of price discrimination under Section 2(a) shall be deemed rebutted where the seller shows "that his lower price or the furnishing of services or facilities to any purchaser or purchasers was made in good faith to meet an equally low price of a competitor, or the services or facilities furnished by a competitor." [15 U.S.C. §13(b)]

Section 2(c). Unlawful Brokerage. Prohibits the payment, in connection with interstate transactions, of brokerage commissions or discounts in lieu of brokerage to, or the receipt of such compensation from, the other party to a transaction or his agent. Does not apply to brokerage commissions paid by a principal to its agent for services rendered by the latter to the principal. [15 U.S.C. §13(c)]

Section 2(d). Payments for Services Furnished by Customers. Prohibits a seller, in connection with interstate transactions, from paying anything of value to or for the benefit of any customer as compensation for any services rendered by such customer in connection with the "processing, handling, sale, or offering for sale" of the seller's products unless such payment "is available on proportionally equal terms to all other customers competing in the distribution of such products." [15 U.S.C. §13(d)]

Section 2(e). Furnishing of Services or Facilities to Customers. Prohibits a seller, in connection with interstate transactions, from furnishing to any purchaser "services or facilities connected with the processing, handling, sale, or offering for sale of [the seller's products] upon terms not accorded to all purchasers on proportionally equal terms." [15 U.S.C. §13(e)]

Section 2(f). Buyer Liability. Prohibits "any person engaged in commerce, in the course of such commerce, knowingly to induce or receive a discrimination in price which is prohibited by [Section 2(a)]." [15 U.S.C. §13(f)]

100

FEDERAL TRADE COMMISSION ACT
(Enacted in 1914)

Section 5(a)(1). Unfair Methods of Competition, etc. Declares unlawful "unfair methods of competition in or affecting commerce, and unfair or deceptive acts or practices in or affecting commerce."** [15 U.S.C. §45(a)(1)]

WILSON TARIFF ACT OF 1894

Section 73. Restraints of Import Trade. Declares illegal and void "every combination, conspiracy, trust, agreement, or contract . . . between two or more persons or corporations, either of whom, as agent or principal, is engaged in importing any article from any foreign country into the United States, and when such combination, conspiracy, trust, agreement, or contract is intended to operate in restraint of lawful trade, or free competition in lawful trade or commerce, or to increase the market price in any part of the United States of any article or articles imported or intended to be imported into the United States, or of any manufacture into which such imported article enters or is intended to enter." [15 U.S.C. §8]

REVENUE ACT OF 1916

Section 801. Antidumping. Provides "that it shall be unlawful for any person importing or assisting in importing any articles from any foreign country into the United States, commonly and systematically to import, sell or cause to be imported or sold such articles within the United States at a price substantially less than the actual market value or wholesale price of such articles, at the time of exportation to the United States, in the principal markets of the country of their production, or of other foreign countries to which they are commonly exported, after adding to such market value or wholesale price, freight, duty, and other charges and expenses necessarily incident to the importation and sale thereof in the United States: *Provided,* That such act or acts be done, with the intent of destroying or injuring an industry in the United States, or of preventing the establishment of an industry in the United States, or of restraining or monopolizing any part of trade and commerce in such articles in the United States." [15 U.S.C. §72]

ANTIDUMPING ACT OF 1921

*Section 160.*** Dumping Investigation.* Provides that if the Secretary of the Treasury determines that a class or kind of foreign merchandise is being, or is likely to be, sold in the United States or elsewhere at less than its fair value, and the United States International Trade Commission thereafter determines that a domestic industry is being, or is likely to be, injured, or is prevented from being established, by reason of the importation of such merchandise into the United States, the Secretary shall make public a notice of his and the Commission's determinations. [19 U.S.C. §160]

Section 161. Special Dumping Duty. Provides for the assessment of a special dumping duty, under certain specified terms and conditions, on imported merchandise of the class or kind as to which the Secretary has made a public finding as provided for in Section 160. [19 U.S.C. §161]

TARIFF ACT OF 1930

*Section 337(a).*** Unfair Methods of Competition in Import Trade.* "Unfair methods of competition and unfair acts in the importation of articles into the United States, or in their sale by the owner, importer, consignee, or agent of either, the effect or tendency of which is to destroy or substantially injure an industry, efficiently and economically operated, in the United States, or to prevent the establishment of such an industry, or to restrain or monopolize the trade and commerce in the United States, are declared unlawful." [19 U.S.C. §1337(a)]

Section 337 is enforced by the United States International Trade Commission which, upon finding a violation, can order exclusion of the article concerned from entry into the United States or discontinuance of the unfair methods or acts involved. The Commission's actions can be nullified by the President. Exclusion orders, if not nullified by the President, are reviewable by the United States Court of Customs and Patent Appeals.

*The Miller-Tydings Amendment, excepting from the Sherman Act resale price maintenance contracts lawful under state laws, was repealed effective March 11, 1976.

**The McGuire Amendment, excepting from the Federal Trade Commission Act and the antitrust laws resale price maintenance contracts lawful under state laws, and the enforcement of such contracts against nonsigners as well as signers thereof, was repealed effective March 11, 1976.

***As amended by the Trade Act of 1974.

Biographies of Authors

BETTY BOCK: Director, Antitrust Research
The Conference Board

> Adjunct Professor of Law, New York University School of Law; Member, Board of Advisors, Columbia University Center for Law and Economic Studies; Adjunct Member, Committee on Trade Regulation, Bar Association of the City of New York; consultant to the General Accounting Office; Member, Advisory Board, *The Antitrust Bulletin.*

KENNETH W. DAM: Professor Law
University of Chicago

> Member, American Bar Association, New York State Bar Association, American Law Institute. Formerly Executive Director, Council on Economic Policy, The White House; Assistant Director, Office of Management and Budget. Author of books and articles on law and economic aspects of antitrust and government regulation.

ALLEN C. HOLMES: Jones, Day, Reavis & Pogue
Cleveland, Ohio

> Member, Council, American Bar Association Section of Antitrust Law; Member, American Bar Association, Ohio State Bar Association, The Association of the Bar of the City of New York, Cleveland Bar Association, American Law Institute; Board of Directors, Sherwin-Williams Company, National City Bank and National City Corporation, of Cleveland, Ohio. Formerly Chairman, Federal Trade Commission Committee, American Bar Association Section of Antitrust Law.

MILES W. KIRKPATRICK: Morgan, Lewis & Bockius
Washington, D.C.

> Chairman, President's Commission on White House Fellowships; Member, American Bar Association, Pennsylvania Bar Association, Philadelphia Bar Association. Formerly Chairman, Federal Trade Commission; American Bar Association Section of Antitrust Law; American Bar Association Commission to Study the Federal Trade Commission.

PAUL H. LaRUE: Chadwell, Kayser, Ruggles, McGee & Hastings
Chicago, Illinois

>Chairman, Robinson-Patman Act Committee, American Bar Association Section of Antitrust Law; Member, Advisory Board, *The Antitrust Bulletin*. Formerly Chairman, Committee on Antitrust Law, Chicago Bar Association; Chairman of Robinson-Patman Act Monograph Project of American Bar Association Section of Antitrust Law; trial attorney and legal advisor to a Commissioner, Federal Trade Commission.

IRA M. MILLSTEIN: Weil, Gotshal & Manges
New York, New York

>Adjunct Professor of Law, New York University School of Law; Member, American Bar Association Section of Antitrust Law; Section Delegate to the American Bar Association House of Delegates; Chairman, Committee on Ratemaking and Economic Regulation, Administrative Conference of the United States; Member, Advisory Board. BNA *Antitrust & Trade Regulation Report.* Formerly Chairman, National Commission on Consumer Finance; Member, National Institute for Consumer Justice. Author and lecturer on antitrust subjects.

ROBERT A. NITSCHKE: Assistant General Counsel
General Motors Corporation

>Formerly Chief, Cartel and Patent Section, Antitrust Division, and Special Assistant to the Attorney General, U.S. Department of Justice; Member, Council, American Bar Association Section of Antitrust Law; Chairman, Committee on Extraterritorial Application of the Antitrust Laws, American Bar Association Section of Antitrust Law. Author of several articles in the antitrust field.

JAMES A. RAHL: Dean, School of Law
Northwestern University

>Counsel, Chadwell, Kayser, Ruggles, McGee & Hastings, Chicago, Illinois. Formerly resident partner, Brussels, Belgium office of Chadwell, Keck, Kayser & Ruggles; Member, Group of Experts on International Restrictive Trade Practices, United Nations Committee on Trade and Development; White House Task Force on Antitrust Policy; Attorney General's National Committee to Study the Antitrust Laws.

FREDERICK M. ROWE: Kirkland, Ellis & Rowe
Washington, D.C.

>Formerly Chairman, American Bar Association Section of Antitrust Law; Member, American Bar Association Commission to Study the Federal Trade Commission; Chairman, Council on Antitrust and

Trade Regulation, Federal Bar Association; Conferee on Antitrust Policy in Distribution, Attorney General's National Committee to Study the Antitrust Laws. Author of *Price Discrimination Under the Robinson-Patman Act,* 1962, with 1964 Supplement; and numerous publications on trade regulation problems.

HOWARD L. SIERS: Assistant Comptroller
E.I. du Pont de Nemours & Company

Member, Financial Executives Institute.

PETER O. STEINER: Professor of Economics and Law
University of Michigan

Formerly Visiting Professor of Economics, University of Nairobi, Kenya; Faculty Research Fellow of the Social Science Research Council; Guggenheim Fellow; Ford Foundation Faculty Research Fellow. Author of *Mergers: Motives, Effects, and Policies,* 1975; and other books and articles.

JAMES H. WALLACE, JR.: Kirkland, Ellis & Rowe
Washington, D.C.

Chairman, Patent, Trademark and Know-How Committee, American Bar Association Section of Antitrust Law; Member, The Bureau of National Affairs, Inc. Patent, Trademark and Copyright Journal Advisory Board. Formerly Attorney, Antitrust Division, U.S. Department of Justice; Examiner, U.S. Patent Office.

A. PAUL VICTOR: Weil, Gotshal & Manges
New York, New York

Chairman, Subcommittee on International Unfair Competition, American Bar Association Section of Antitrust Law; Member, New York State Bar Association. Formerly attorney, Antitrust Division, U.S. Department of Justice.

Related Publications of The Conference Board

Papers from Recent Antitrust Conferences
Sponsored by The Conference Board

Antitrust in a Rapidly Changing Economy: Large-Scale Investments and Competition, Papers from the Fourteenth Conference on Antitrust Issues in Today's Economy, March 6, 1975.

> Explores the relations between large-scale investments and competition and examines some of the strands of antitrust in a rapidly changing economy. Addresses by Robert M. Estes and Almarin Phillips and a dialogue among Frederick M. Rowe, Donald I. Baker, and Allen C. Holmes.

Antitrust and Shifting National Controls Policies, Transcript of Thirteenth Conference on Antitrust Issues in Today's Economy, March 7, 1974.

> Examines the impact on differently positioned companies of the shifting relations between antitrust and conflicting or complementary national controls policies. Addresses by Robert L. Werner and Neil H. Jacoby and dialogue among Frederick M. Rowe, M.A. Adelman, and Louis B. Schwartz.

Antitrust in Search of an Identity: Images and Classical Models Under Cross-fire, Transcript of Twelfth Conference on Antitrust Issues in Today's Economy, March 1, 1973.

> Examines some of the relations between the classical economic models underlying decisions under the antitrust laws and the factual economic problems of the 1970's; also explores the role and limits of the trade regulation laws as tools for social change. Addresses by Eugene M. Singer and Ira M. Millstein and dialogue among Frederick M. Rowe, Victor H. Kramer, and Paul C. Warnke.

Antitrust Problems and National Priorities: Competitive Measures and Competitive Facts, Transcript of Eleventh Conference on Antitrust Issues in Today's Economy, March 2, 1972.

> Explores questions concerning economic policy, national goals, and antitrust issues in terms of natural priorities and national economic programs. Addresses by Walter Adams, Howard J. Aibel, and Simon Ramo.

Economic Fact and Antitrust Goals: Inputs for Corporate Planning, Transcript of Tenth Conference on Antitrust Issues in Today's Economy, March 11, 1971.

Explores corporate management options and the problems of advising corporate management concerning modern technologies and competition. Addresses by Daniel Walker, Howard Adler, Jr., Nestor E. Terleckyj, Allen C. Holmes, and Bernard G. Segal.

New Technologies, Competition, and Antitrust: Consequences of Multiplying Company and Market Structures, Transcript of Ninth Conference on Antitrust Issues in Today's Economy, March 5, 1970.

Examines the consequences for antitrust of multiplying company and market structures; it deals with problems of successful companies, changing environments and new concepts of firms and markets, and antitrust questions raised by vanishing boundaries. Addresses by Francis R. Kirkham, J. Fred Weston, Glen McDaniel, Richard W. McLaren, and Frederick M. Rowe.

Recent Antitrust Studies and Articles
  by The Conference Board

"New Numbers on Concentration: Fears and Facts," *The Conference Board Record,* March 1976.

"Consistency and Change in Antitrust," *The Conference Board Record,* February 1976.

"Line-of-Business Reporting: A Quest for a Snark?," *The Conference Board Record,* November 1975.

"Concentration as an Economic Scapegoat," *The Conference Board Record,* June 1975.

"Notes on the Future of Competition: Can We Afford an Economy of Choice?," *The Conference Board Record*, March 1975.

"From Administered Pricing to Concentrated Market Pricing," *The Conference Board Record*, February 1975.

Line-of-Business Reporting: Problems in the Formulation of a Data Program," Conference Board Report No. 654, 1975.

Restructuring Proposals: Measuring Competition in Numerical Grids, Conference Board Report No. 619, 1974.

An Anthology of Studies of Industrial Concentration by The Conference Board: 1958-1972, 1973.

Dialogue on Concentration, Oligopoly, and Profit: Concepts vs. Data, Conference Board Report No. 556, 1972.